Books by Galway Kinnell

A New
Selected
Poems

GALWAY KINNELL

A Mariner Book

HOUGHTON MIFFLIN COMPANY

Boston   New York

First Mariner Books edition 2001

Copyright © 2000, 2001 by Galway Kinnell

Library of Congress Cataloging-in-Publication Data

Kinnell, Galway, date.
[Poems. Selections]
A new selected poetry / Galway Kinnell.
p. cm.
ISBN 0-618-02187-6
ISBN 0-618-15445-0 (pbk.)
I. Title.
PS3521.I582 A6 2000
811'.54—dc21   99-048904

Book design by Anne Chalmers
Typeface: Electra

Printed in the United States of America

QUM 10 9 8 7

To EPHRAIM and MIRAH

O yonge, fresshe folkes, he or she,
In which that love upgroweth with youre age
. . . thynketh al nys but a faire
This world, that passeth soone as floures faire.
                    —Chaucer

Contents

FROM When One Has Lived a Long Time Alone 1990

FROM Imperfect Thirst 1994

Author's Note

In this paperback edition of A *New Selected Poems*, I have taken out three poems, all from early books, that were included in the hardcover edition, and added eight others, mostly from later books. This edition also incorporates revisions that were not present in the hardcover book. For many years, I have felt exasperated by my intractable habit of working at certain poems again and again, over long spans of time. But in recent years I have come to accept that, at least in the case of a complex project, this is simply how I write. It makes me think of the digestive process of a Methuselah-ian ruminant animal, one with many many stomachs, that chews its cud for decades (though I don't want to carry this analogy to its logical alimentary end). From the outside, it may seem only that a given poem has been belatedly revised, while to me, making these changes was still part of the process of composition, a final stage in the protracted struggle with my very "sullen art."

I would like to thank my peerless editor, Pat Strachan; Janet Silver, editor in chief; and Wendy Strothman, executive vice president, all of Houghton Mifflin, for understanding how necessary these reworkings are to me in my effort to bring the poems into their final form.

What a Kingdom It Was

1960

First Song

Then it was dusk in Illinois, the small boy
After an afternoon of carting dung
Hung on the rail fence, a sapped thing
Weary to crying. Dark was growing tall
And he began to hear the pond frogs all
Calling on his ear with what seemed their joy.

Soon their sound was pleasant for a boy
Listening in the smoky dusk and the nightfall
Of Illinois, and from the fields two small
Boys came bearing cornstalk violins
And they rubbed the cornstalk bows with resins
And the three sat there scraping of their joy.

It was now fine music the frogs and the boys
Did in the towering Illinois twilight make
And into dark in spite of a shoulder's ache
A boy's hunched body loved out of a stalk
The first song of his happiness, and the song woke
His heart to the darkness and into the sadness of joy.

For William Carlos Williams

When you came and you talked and you read with your
Private zest from the varicose marble
Of the podium, the lovers of literature
Paid you the tribute of their almost total
Inattention, although someone when you spoke of a pig
Did squirm, and it is only fair to report another gig-

gled. But you didn't even care. You seemed
Above remarking we were not your friends.
You hung around inside the rimmed
Circles of your heavy glasses and smiled and
So passed a lonely evening. In an hour
Of talking your honesty built you a tower.

When it was over and you sat down and the chair-
man got up and smiled and congratulated
You and shook your hand, I watched a professor
In neat bow tie and enormous tweeds, who patted
A faint praise of the sufficiently damned,
Drained spittle from his pipe, then scrammed.

Freedom, New Hampshire

1

We came to visit the cow
Dying of fever,
Towle said it was already
Shoveled under, in a secret
Burial-place in the woods.
We prowled through the woods
Weeks, we never

Found where. Other
Children other summers
Must have found the place
And asked, Why is it
Green here? The rich
Guess a grave, maybe,
The poor think a pit

For dung, like the one
We shoveled in in the fall,
That came up a brighter green
The next year, that
Could as well have been
The grave of a cow
Or something, for all that shows.

2

We found a cowskull once; we thought it was
From one of the asses in the Bible, for the sun
Shone into the holes through which it had seen
Earth as an endless belt carrying gravel, had heard
Its truculence cursed, had learned how human sweat
Stinks, and had brayed—shone into the holes
With solemn and majestic light, as if some
Skull somewhere could be Baalbek or the Parthenon.

That night passing Towle's Barn
We saw lights. Towle had lassoed a calf
By its hind legs, and he tugged against the grip
Of the darkness. The cow stood by, chewing millet.
Derry and I took hold, too, and hauled.
It was sopping with darkness when it came free.
It was a bullcalf. The cow mopped it awhile,
And we walked around it with a lantern,

And it was sunburned, somehow, and beautiful.
It took a teat as the first business
And sneezed and drank at the milk of light.
When we got it balanced on its legs, it went wobbling
Toward the night. Walking home in darkness
We saw the July moon looking on Freedom, New Hampshire,
We smelled the fall in the air, it was the summer,
We thought, Oh this is but the summer!

3

Once I saw the moon
Drift into the sky like a bright
Pregnancy pared
From a goddess who had to
Keep slender to remain beautiful—
Cut loose, and drifting up there
To happen by itself—
And waning, in lost labor;

As we lost our labor
Too—afternoons
When we sat on the gate
By the pasture, under the Ledge,
Buzzing and skirling on toilet-
papered combs tunes
To the rumble-seated cars
Taking the Ossipee Road

On Sundays; for
Though dusk would come upon us

Where we sat, and though we had
Skirled out our hearts in the music,
Yet the not-yet dandruffed
Harps we skirled it on
Had done not much better than
Flies, which buzzed, when quick

We trapped them in our hands,
Which went silent when we
Crushed them, which we bore
Downhill to the meadowlark's
Nest full of throats, which
Derry charmed and combed
With an Arabian air, while I
Chucked crushed flies into

Innards I could not see,
For the night had fallen
And the crickets shrilled on all sides
In waves, as if the grassleaves
Shrieked by hillsides
As they grew, and the stars
Made small flashes in the sky,
Like mica flashing in rocks

On the chokecherried Ledge
Where bees I stepped on once
Hit us from behind like a shotgun,
And where we could see
Windowpanes in Freedom flash
And Loon Lake and Winnipesaukee
Flash in the sun
And the blue world flashing.

4

The fingerprints of our eyeballs would zigzag
On the sky; the clouds that came drifting up
Our fingernails would drift into the thin air;
In bed at night there was music if you listened,
Of an old surf breaking far away in the blood.

7

Children who come by chance on grass green for a man
Can guess cow, dung, man, anything they want,
To them it is the same. To us who knew him as he was
After the beginning and before the end, it is green
For a name called out of the confusions of the earth—

Winnipesaukee coined like a moon, a bullcalf
Dragged from the darkness where it breaks up again,
Larks which long since have crashed for good in the grass
To which we fed the flies, buzzing ourselves like flies,
While the crickets shrilled beyond us, in July.

The mind may sort it out and give it names—
When a man dies he dies trying to say without slurring
The abruptly decaying sounds. It is true
That only flesh dies, and spirit flowers without stop
For men, cows, dung, for all dead things; and it is good, yes—

But an incarnation is in particular flesh
And the dust that is swirled into a shape
And crumbles and is swirled again had but one shape
That was this man. When he is dead the grass
Heals what he suffered, but he remains dead,
And the few who loved him know this until they die.

For my brother, 1925–1957

The Supper After the Last

1

The desert moves out on half the horizon
Rimming the illusory water which, among islands,
Bears up the sky. The sea scumbles in
From its own inviolate border under the sky.
A dragon-fly floating on six legs on the sand
Lifts its green-yellow tail, declines its wings
A little, flutters them a little, and lays
On dazzled sand the shadow of its wings. Near shore
A bather wades through his shadow in the water.
He tramples and kicks it; it recomposes.

2

Outside the open door
Of the whitewashed house,
Framed in the doorway, a chair,
Vacant, waits in the sunshine.

A jug of fresh water stands
Inside the door. In the sunshine
The chair waits, less and less vacant.
The host's plan is to offer water, then stand aside.

3

They eat chicken, drink rosé. The chicken head
Has been tucked under the shelter of the wing.
Under the table a red-backed, passionate dog
Cracks chicken bones on the blood and gravel floor.

No one else but the dog and the blind
Cat watching it knows who is that bearded
Wild man guzzling overhead, the wreck of passion
Emptying his eyes, who has not yet smiled,

Who stares at the company, where he is company,
Turns them to sacks of appalled, grinning skin,
Forks the fowl-eye out from under
The large, makeshift, cooked lid, evaporates the wine,

Jellies the sunlit table and spoons, floats
The deluxe grub down the intestines of the Styx,
Devours all but the cat, to whom he slips scraps, and the dog,
The red-backed accomplice busy grinding gristle.

4

When the bones of the host
Crack in the hound's jaw
The wild man rises. Opening
His palms he announces:
I came not to astonish
But to destroy you. Your
Jug of cool water? Your
Hanker after wings? Your
Lech for transcendence?
I came to prove you are
Intricate and simple things
As you are, created
In the image of nothing,
Taught of the creator
By your images in dirt—
As mine, for which you set
A chair in the sunshine,
Mocking me with water!
As pictures of wings,
Not even iridescent,
That clasp the sand
And that cannot perish, you swear,
Having once been evoked!

5

The witnesses back off; the scene begins to float in water.
Far out in that mirage the Savior sits whispering to the world,
Becoming a mirage. The dog turns into a smear on the sand.
The cat grows taller and taller as it flees into space.

From the hot shine where he sits his whispering drifts:
You struggle from flesh into wings; the change exists.
But the wings that live gripping the contours of the dirt
Are all at once nothing, flesh and light lifted away.

You are the flesh; I am the resurrection, because I am the light.
I cut to your measure the creeping piece of darkness
That haunts you everywhere under the sun. Step into light —
I make you over. I breed the shape of your grave in the dirt.

The Avenue Bearing the Initial of Christ into the New World

Was diese kleine Gasse doch für ein Reich an sich war . . .

1

pcheek pcheek pcheek pcheek pcheek
They cry. The motherbirds thieve the air
To appease them. A tug on the East River
Blasts the bass-note of its passage, lifted
From the infra-bass of the sea. A broom
Swishes over the sidewalk like feet through leaves.
Valerio's pushcart Ice Coal Kerosene
Moves   clack
           clack
               clack
On a broken wheelrim. Ringing in its chains
The New Star Laundry horse comes down the street
Like a roofleak whucking into a pail.
At the redlight, where a horn blares,
The Golden Harvest Bakery brakes on its gears,
Squeaks, and seethes in place. A propane-
gassed bus makes its way with big, airy sighs.

Across the street a woman throws open
Her window,
She sets, terribly softly,
Two potted plants on the windowledge
           tic   tic
And bangs shut her window.

A man leaves a doorway tic toc tic toc tic toc tic hurrah toc splat
      on Avenue C tic etc and turns the corner.
Banking the same corner
A pigeon coasts 5th Street in shadows,
Looks for altitude, surmounts the rims of buildings,
And turns white.

The babybirds pipe down. It is day.

2

In sunlight on the Avenue
The Jew rocks along in a black fur shtraimel,
Black robe, black knickers, black knee-stockings,
Black shoes. His beard like a sod-bottom
Hides the place where he wears no tie.
A dozen children troop after him, barbels flying,
In skullcaps. They are Reuben, Simeon, Levi, Judah, Issachar,
    Zebulun, Benjamin, Dan, Naphtali, Gad, Asher.
With the help of the Lord they will one day become
Courtiers, thugs, rulers, rabbis, asses, adders, wrestlers, bakers,
    poets, cartpushers, infantrymen.

The old man is sad-faced. He is near burial
And one son is missing. The women who bore him sons
And are past bearing, mourn for the son
And for the father, wondering if the man will go down
Into the grave of a son mourning, or if at the last
The son will put his hands on the eyes of his father.

The old man wades toward his last hour.
On 5th Street, between Avenues A and B,
In sunshine, in his private cloud, Bunko Certified Embalmer,
Cigar in his mouth, nose to the wind, leans
At the doorway of Bunko's Funeral Home & Parlour,
Glancing west toward the Ukrainians, eastward idly
Where the Jew rocks toward his last hour.

Sons, grandsons at his heel, the old man
Confronts the sun. He does not feel its rays
Through his beard, he does not understand
Fruits and vegetables live by the sun.
Like his children he is sallow-faced, he sees
A blinding signal in the sky, he smiles.

Bury me not Bunko damned Catholic I pray you in Egypt.

3

From the Station House
Under demolishment on Houston
To the Power Station on 14th,
Jews, blacks, Puerto Ricans
Walk in the spring sunlight.

The Downtown Talmud Torah
Blosztein's Cutrate Bakery
Areceba Panataria Hispano
Peanuts Dried Fruit Nuts & Canned Goods
Productos Tropicales
Appetizing Herring Candies Nuts
Nathan Kugler Chicken Store Fresh Killed Daily
Little Rose Restaurant
Rubinstein the Hatter Mens Boys Hats Caps Furnishings
J. Herrmann Dealer in All Kinds of Bottles
Natural Bloom Cigars
Blony Bubblegum
Mueren las Cucarachas Super Potente Garantizada de Matar las
    Cucarachas mas Resistentes
Wenig מצבות
G. Schnee Stairbuilder
Everyouth la Original Loción Eterna Juventud Satisfacción Dinero
    Devuelto
Happy Days Bar & Grill

Through dust-stained windows over storefronts,
Curtains drawn aside, onto the Avenue
Thronged with Puerto Ricans, blacks, Jews,
Baby carriages stuffed with groceries and babies,
The old women peer, blessed damozels
Sitting up there young forever in the cockroached rooms,
Eating fresh-killed chicken, productos tropicales,
Appetizing herring, canned goods, nuts;
They puff out smoke from Natural Bloom cigars
And one day they puff like Blony Bubblegum.

From a rooftop a boy fishes at the sky,
Around him a flock of pigeons fountains,

Blown down and swirling up again, seeking the sky.
A red kite wriggles like a tadpole
Into the sky beyond them, crosses
The sun, lays bare its own crossed skeleton.

To fly from this place—to roll
On some bubbly blacktop in the summer,
To run under the rain of pigeon plumes, to be
Tarred, and feathered with birdshit, Icarus,

In Kugler's glass headdown dangling by yellow legs.

4

First Sun Day of the year. Tonight,
When the sun will have turned from the earth,
She will appear outside Hy's Luncheonette,
The crone who sells the *News* and the *Mirror*,
The oldest living thing on Avenue C,
Outdating much of its brick and mortar.
If you ask for the *News* she gives you the *Mirror*
And squints long at the nickel in her hand
Despising it, perhaps, for being a nickel,
And stuffs it in her apron pocket
And sucks her lips. Rain or stars, every night
She is there, squatting on the orange crate,
Issuing out only in darkness, like the cucarachas
And dread nightmares in the chambers overhead.
She can't tell one newspaper from another,
She has forgotten how Nain her dead husband looked,
She has forgotten her children's whereabouts,
Or how many there were, or what the *News*
And *Mirror* tell about that we buy them with nickels.
She is sure only of the look of a nickel
And that there is a Lord in the sky overhead.
She dwells in a flesh that is of the Lord
And drifts out, therefore, only in darkness,
Like the streetlamp outside the Luncheonette
Or the lights in the secret chamber
In the firmament, where Yahweh himself dwells.

Like Magdalene in the Battistero of Saint John
On the carved-up continent, in the land of sun,
She lives shadowed, under a feeble bulb
That lights her face, her crab's hands, her small bulk on the crate.

She is Pulchería mother of murderers and madmen,
She is also Alyona whose neck was a chicken leg.

Mother was it the insufferable wind?
She sucks her lips a little further into the mousehole.
She stares among the stars, and among the streetlamps.

The mystery is hers.

5
That violent song of the twilight!
Now, in the silence, will the motherbirds
Be dead, and the infantbirds
That were in the dawn merely transparent
Unfinished things, nothing but bellies,
Will they have been shoved out
And in the course of a morning, casually,
On scrawny wings, have taken up the life?

6
In the pushcart market, on Sunday,
A crate of lemons discharges light like a battery.
Icicle-shaped carrots that through black soil
Wove away lie like flames in the sun.
Onions with their shirts ripped seek sunlight
On green skins. The sun beats
On beets dirty as boulders in cowfields,
On turnips pinched and gibbous
From budging rocks, on embery sweets,
On Idahos, Long Islands, and Maines,
On horseradishes still growing weeds on the flat ends,
On cabbages lying about like sea-green brains
The skulls have been shucked from,

On tomatoes, undented plum-tomatoes, alligator-skinned
Cucumbers, that float pickled
In the wooden tubs of green skim milk—

Sky-flowers, dirt-flowers, underdirt-flowers,
Those that climbed for the sun in their lives
And those that wormed away—equally uprooted,
Maimed, lopped, shucked, and misaimed.

In the market in Damascus a goat
Came to a stall where twelve goatheads
Were lined up for sale. It sniffed them
One by one. Finally thirteen goats started
Smiling in their faintly sardonic way.

A crone buys a pickle from a crone,
It is wrapped in the *Mirror*,
At home she will open the wrapping, stained,
And stare and stare and stare at it.

And the cucumbers, and the melons,
And the leeks, and the onions, and the garlic.

7

Already the Avenue troughs the light of day.
Southward, toward Houston and Pitt,
Where Avenue C begins, the eastern ranges
Of the wiped-out lives—punks, lushes,
Panhandlers, pushers, rumsoaks, all those
Who took it easy when they should have been out failing at
        something—
The pots-and-pans man pushes his cart,
Through the intersection of the light, at 3rd,
Where sunset smashes on the aluminum of it,
On the bottoms, curves, handles, metal panes,
Mirrors: of the bead-curtained cave under the falls
In Freedom, Seekonk Woods leafing the light out,
Halfway to Kingston where a road branched out suddenly,
Between Pamplonne and Les Salins two meeting paths

Over a sea the green of churchsteeple copper.
Of all places on earth inhabited by men
Why is it we find ourselves on this Avenue
Where the dusk gets worse,
And the mirrorman pushing his heaped mirrors
Into the shadows between 3rd and 2nd
Pushes away a mess of old pots and pans?

The ancient black man sits as usual
Outside the Happy Days Bar & Grill. He wears
Dark glasses. Every once in a while, abruptly,
He starts to sing, chanting in a hoarse, nearly breaking
Voice —

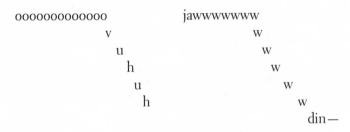

And becomes silent
      Stares into the polaroid Wilderness
Gross-Rosen, Maidanek, Flössenberg, Ravensbruck, Stutthof, Riga,
Bergen-Belsen, Mauthausen, Birkenau, Treblinka, Natzweiler,
Dachau, Buchenwald, Auschwitz —
                    Villages,
Pasture-bordered hamlets on the far side of the river.

8

The promise was broken too freely
To them and to their fathers, for them to care.
They survive like cedars on a cliff, roots
Hooked in any crevice they can find.
They walk Avenue C in shadows
Neither conciliating its Baalim
Nor whoring after landscapes of the senses,
Tarig bab el Amoud being in the blood

Fumigated by Puerto Rican cooking.
Among women girthed like cedar trees
Other, slenderer ones appear:
One yellow haired, in August,
Under shooting stars on the lake, who
Believed in promises that broke by themselves—
In a German flower garden in the Bronx
The wedding of a child and a child, one flesh
Divided in the Adirondack spring—
One who found in the desert city of the West
The first happiness, and fled therefore—
And by a southern sea, in the pines, one loved
Until the mist rose blue in the trees
Around the spiderwebs that kept on shining,
Each day of the shortening summer.

And as rubbish burns
And the pushcarts are loaded
With fruits and vegetables and empty crates
And clank away on iron wheels over cobblestones,
And merchants infold their stores
And the carp ride motionlessly sleeplessly
In the dark tank in the fishmarket,
The figures withdraw into chambers overhead—
In the city of the mind, chambers built
Of care and necessity, where, hands lifted to the blinds,
They glimpse in mirrors backed with the blackness of the world
Awkward, cherished rooms containing the familiar selves.

9

Children set fires in ashbarrels,
Cats prowl the fires, scraps of fishes burn.

A child lay in the flames.
It was not the plan. Abraham
Stood in terror at the duplicity.
Isaac whom he loved lay in the flames.
The Lord turned away washing
His hands without soap and water

Like a common housefly.
The children laugh.
Isaac means *he laughs.*
Maybe the last instant,
The dying itself, *is* easier,
Easier anyway than the hike
From Pitt the blind gut
To the East River of Fishes,
Maybe it is as the poet said,
And the soul turns to thee
O vast and well-veiled Death
And the body gratefully nestles close to thee—

I think of Isaac reading Whitman in Chicago,
The week before he died, coming across
Such a passage and muttering, Oi!
What shit! And smiling, but not for you—I mean,

For *thee*, Sane and Sacred Death!

10

It was Gold's junkhouse, the one the clacking
Carts that little men pad after in harnesses
Picking up bedbugged mattresses, springs
The stubbornness has been loved out of,
Chairs felled by fat, lampshades lights have burned through,
Linoleum the geometry has been scuffed from,
Carriages a single woman's work has brought to wreck,
Would come to in the dusk and unload before,
That the whole neighborhood came out to see
Burning in the night, flames opening out like
Eyelashes from the windows, men firing the tears in,
Searchlights smashing against the brick,
The water blooming up the walls
Like pale trees, reaching into the darkness beyond.

Nobody mourned, nobody stood around in pajamas
And a borrowed coat steaming his nose in coffee.
It was only Gold's junkhouse.
                                    But this evening

The neighborhood comes out again, everything
That may abide the fire was made to go through the fire
And it was made clean: a few twisted springs,
Charred mattresses (crawling still, naturally),
Perambulator skeletons, bicycles tied in knots—
In a great black pile at the junkhouse door,
Smelling of burnt rubber and hair. Rustwater
Hangs in icicles over the windows and door,
Like frozen piss aimed at trespassers,
Combed by wind, set overnight. Carriages we were babies in,
Springs that used to resist love, that gave in
And were thrown out like whores—the black
Irreducible heap, mausoleum of what we were—
It is cold suddenly, we feel chilled,
Nobody knows for sure what is left of him.

11

The fishmarket closed, the fishes gone into flesh.
The smelts draped on each other, fat with roe,
The marble cod hacked into chunks on the counter,
Butterfishes mouths still open, still trying to eat,
Porgies with receding jaws hinged apart
In a grimace of dejection, as if like cows
They had died under the sledgehammer, perches
In grass-green armor, spotted squeteagues
In the melting ice meek-faced and croaking no more,
Mud-eating mullets buried in crushed ice,
Tilefishes with scales like bits of chickenfat,
Spanish mackerels with buttercups on the flanks,
Pot-bellied pikes, two-tone flounders
After the long contortion of pushing both eyes
To the brown side that they might look up,
Lying brown side down, like a mass laying-on of hands,
Or the oath-taking of an army.

The only things alive are the carp
That drift in the black tank in the rear,
Kept living for the usual reason, that they have not died,
And perhaps because the last meal was garbage and they might begin
    smelling

On dying, before the customer got halfway home.
They nudge each other, to be netted,
The sweet flesh to be lifted thrashing into the air,
To be slugged, and then to keep on living
While they are opened on the counter.

Fishes do not die exactly, it is more
That they go out of themselves, the visible part
Remains the same, there is little pallor,
Only the cataracted eyes that have not shut ever
Must look through the mist that crazed Homer.

These are the vegetables of the deep,
The Sheol-flowers of darkness, swimmers
Of denser darknesses where the sun's rays bend for the last time
And in the sky there burns this shifty jellyfish
That degenerates and flashes and re-forms.

Fishes are nailed to the wood,
The fishmonger stands like Christ, nailing them to the wood,
He scrapes the knife up the grain, the scales fly,
He unnails them, reverses them, nails them again,
Scrapes and the scales fly. He lops off the heads,
Shakes out the guts as if they did not belong in the first place,
And they are flesh for the first time in their lives.

Dear Frau _____:
    Your husband, _____, died in the Camp Hospital on _____.
May I express my sincere sympathy on your bereavement. _____ was
admitted to the Hospital on _____ with severe symptoms of
exhaustion, complaining of difficulties in breathing and pains in the
chest. Despite competent medication and devoted medical attention, it
proved impossible, unfortunately, to keep the patient alive. The deceased
voiced no final requests.
                                        Camp Commandant, _____

On 5th Street Bunko Certified Embalmer Catholic
Leans in his doorway drawing on a Natural Bloom Cigar.
He looks up the street. Even the Puerto Ricans are Jews
And the Chinese Laundry closes on Saturday.

12

Next door, outside the pink-fronted Bodega Hispano—

(A crying: you imagine
A baby in its crib, wailing
As if it could foresee everything.
The crying subsides: you imagine
A mother or father clasping
The damned creature in their arms.
It breaks out again, this
Time in a hair-raising shriek—so,
The alleycat, in a pleasant guise,
In the darkness outside, in the alley,
Wauling slowly in its blood.

Another, loftier shrieking
Drowns it out. It begins always
On the high note, over a clang of bells:
Hook & Ladder 11 with an explosion of mufflers
Crab-walking out of 5th Street,
Accelerating up the Avenue, siren
Sliding on the rounded distances,
Returning fainter and fainter,
Like a bee looping away from where you lie in the grass.

The searchlights catch him at the topfloor window,
Trying to move, nailed in place by the shine.

The bells of Saint Brigid's
On Tompkins Square
Toll for someone who has died—
J'oïs la cloche de Serbonne,
Qui tousjours à neuf heures sonne
Le Salut que l'Ange prédit . . .

Expecting the visitation
You lie back on your bed,
The sounds outside
Must be outside. Here
Are only the dead spirituals

Turning back into prayers—
You rise on an elbow
To make sure they come from outside,
You hear nothing, you lay down
Your head on the pillow
Like a pick-up arm—
        swing low
                swing low
                        sweet
        lowsweet—)
—Carols of the Caribbean, plinkings of guitars.

13

The garbage-disposal truck
Like a huge hunched animal
That sucks in garbage in the place
Where other animals evacuate it
Whines, as the cylinder in the rear
Threshes up the trash and garbage,
Where two men in rubber suits
(It must be raining outside)
Heap it in. The whining motor
Deepens to a groan as it grinds in
The garbage, and between-times
Whines. It groans and whines again.
All about it as it moves down
5th Street is the clatter of trashcans,
The crashes of them as the sanitary engineers
Bounce them on the sidewalk.

If it is raining outside
You can only tell by looking
In puddles, under the lifted streetlamps.

It would be the spring rain.

14

Behind the Power Station on 14th, the held breath
Of light, as God is a held breath, withheld,

Spreads the East River, into which fishes leak:
The brown sink or dissolve,
The white float out in shoals and armadas,
Even the gulls pass them up, pale
Bloated socks of riverwater and rotted seed
That swirl on the tide, punched back
To the Hell Gate narrows, and on the ebb
Steam seaward, seeding the sea.

On the Avenue, through air tinted crimson
By neon over the bars, the rain is falling.
You stood once on Houston, among panhandlers and winos
Who weave the eastern ranges, learning to be free,
To not care, to be knocked flat and to get up clear-headed
Spitting the curses out. "Now be nice,"
The proprietor threatens; "Be nice," he cajoles.
"Fuck you," the bum shouts as he is hoisted again,
"God fuck your mother." (In the empty doorway,
Hunched on the empty crate, the crone gives no sign.)

That night a wildcat cab whined crosstown on 7th.
You knew even the traffic lights were made by God,
The red splashes growing dimmer the farther away
You looked, and away up at 14th, a few green stars;
And without sequence, and nearly all at once,
The red lights blinked into green,
And just before there was one complete Avenue of green,
The little green stars in the distance blinked.

It is night, and raining. You look down
Toward Houston in the rain, the living streets,
Where instants of transcendence
Drift in oceans of loathing and fear, like lanternfishes,
Or phosphorous flashings in the sea, or the feverish light
Skin is said to give off when the swimmer drowns at night .

From the blind gut Pitt to the East River of Fishes
The Avenue cobbles a swath through the discolored air,
A roadway of refuse from the teeming shores and ghettos
And the Caribbean Paradise, into the new ghetto and new paradise,
This God-forsaken Avenue bearing the initial of Christ

Through the haste and carelessness of the ages,
The sea standing in heaps, which keeps on collapsing,
Where the drowned suffer a C-change,
And remain the common poor.

Since Providence, for the realization of some unknown purpose, has
seen fit to leave this dangerous people on the face of the earth
and did not destroy it . . .

Listen! the swish of the blood,
The sirens down the bloodpaths of the night,
Bone tapping on the bone, nerve-nets
Singing under the breath of sleep—

We scattered over the lonely seaways,
Over the lonely deserts did we run,
In dark lanes and alleys we did hide ourselves . . .

The heart beats without windows in its night,
The lungs put out the light of the world as they
Heave and collapse, the brain turns and rattles
In its own black axlegrease—

                  In the nighttime
Of the blood they are laughing and saying,
Our little lane, what a kingdom it was!

            oi weih, oi weih

FROM

Flower Herding
on Mount Monadnock

1964

The River That Is East

1

Buoys begin clanging like churches
And peter out. Sunk to the gunwhales
In their shapes, tugs push upstream.
A carfloat booms down, sweeping past
Illusory suns that blaze in puddles
On the shores where it rained, past the Navy Yard,
Under the Williamsburg Bridge
That hangs facedown from its strings
Over which the Jamaica Local crawls,
Through white-winged gulls which shriek
And flap from the water and sideslip in
Over the chaos of illusions, dangling
Limp red hands, and screaming as they touch.

2

A boy swings his legs from the pier,
His days go by. Tugs and carfloats go by,
Each prow pushing a whitecap. On his deathbed
Kane remembered the abrupt, missed Grail
Called Rosebud, Gatsby may have flashed back
To his days digging clams in Little Girl Bay
In Minnesota, Nick fished in dreamy Michigan,
Gant had his memories, Griffiths, those
Who went baying after the immaterial
And whiffed its strange dazzle in a blonde
In a canary convertible, who died
Thinking of the Huck Finns of themselves
On the old afternoons, themselves like this boy
Swinging his legs, who sees the *Ile de France*
Come in, and wonders if in some stateroom
There is not a sick-hearted heiress sitting
Drink in hand, saying to herself his name.

3

A man stands on the pier.
He has long since stopped wishing his heart were full
Or his life dear to him.
He watches the snowfall hitting the dirty water.
He thinks: Beautiful. Beautiful.
If I were a gull I would be one with white wings,
I would fly out over the water, explode, and
Be beautiful snow hitting the dirty water.

4

And thou, River of Tomorrow, flowing . . .
We stand on the shore, which is mist beneath us,
And regard the onflowing river. Sometimes
It seems the river stops and the shore
Flows into the past. What is this river
But the one that drags the things we love,
Processions of debris like floating lamps
Toward the radiance in which they go out?
No, it is the River that is East, known once
From a high window in Brooklyn, in agony — flood
On which a door locked to the water floats,
A window sash paned with brown water, a whiskey crate,
Barrel staves, sun spokes, feathers of the birds,
A breadcrust, a rat, spittle, butts, and peels,
The immaculate stream, heavy, and swinging home again.

For Robert Frost

1

Why do you talk so much
Robert Frost? One day
I drove up to Ripton to ask,

I stayed the whole day
And never got the chance
To put the question.

I drove off at dusk
Worn out and aching
In both ears. Robert Frost,

Were you shy as a boy?
Do you go on making up
For some long period of solitude?

Is it that talk
Doesn't have to be metered and rhymed?
Or is talk distracting from something worse?

2

I saw you once on the TV,
Unsteady at the lectern,
The flimsy white leaf
Of hair standing straight up
In the wind, among top hats,
Old farmer and son
Of worse winters than this,
Stopped in the first dazzle

Of the District of Columbia,
Suddenly having to pay
For the cheap onionskin,

The worn-out ribbon, the eyes
Wrecked from writing poems
For us—stopped,
Lonely before millions,
The paper jumping in your grip,

And as the Presidents
Also on the platform
Began flashing nervously
Their Presidential smiles
For the harmless old guy,
And poets watching on the TV
Started thinking, Well that's
The end of *that* tradition,

And the managers of the event
Said, Boys this is it,
This sonofabitch poet
Is gonna croak,
Putting the paper aside
You drew forth
From your great faithful heart
The poem.

3

Once, walking in winter in Vermont,
In the snow, I followed a set of footprints
That aimed for the woods. At the verge
I could make out, "far in the pillared dark,"
An old creature in a huge, clumsy overcoat,
Lifting his great boots through the drifts,
Going as if to die among "those dark trees"
Of his own country. I watched him go,

Past a house, quiet, warm and light,
A farm, a countryside, a woodpile in its slow
Smokeless burning, alder swamps ghastly white,
Tumultuous snows, blanker whitenesses,
Into the pathless wood, one eye weeping,

The dark trees, for which no saying is dark enough,
Which mask the gloom and lead on into it,
The bare, the withered, the deserted.

There were no more cottages.
Soft bombs of dust falling from the boughs,
The sun shining no warmer than the moon,
He had outwalked the farthest city light,
And there, clinging to the perfect trees,
A last leaf. What was it?
What was that whiteness?—white, uncertain—
The night too dark to know.

4

He turned. *Love,*
Love of things, duty, he said,
And made his way back to the shelter
No longer sheltering him, the house
Where everything turned into words,

Where he would think on the white wave,
Folded back, that rides in place on the obscure
Pouring of this life to the sea—
And seal the broken lips
Of darkness with the *mot juste.*

5

Poet of the country of white houses,
Of clearings going out to the dark wall of woods
Frayed along the skyline, you who nearly foreknew
The next lines of poems you suddenly left off writing,
Who dwelt in access to that which other men
Have burned all their lives to get near, who heard
The high wind, in gusts, seething
From far off, coming through the trees exactly
To this place where it must happen, who spent
Your life on the point of giving yourself away
To the dark trees, the dissolving woods,
Into which you go at last, heart in hand, deep in:

When we think of a man who was cursed
Neither with the all-lovingness of Walt Whitman
Nor with Melville's anguish to know and to suffer,
And yet cursed . . . A man, what shall I say,
Vain, not fully convinced he was dying, whose calling
Was to set up in the wilderness of his country,
At whatever cost, a man who would be his own man,
We think of you. And from the same doorway
At which you lived, between the house and the woods,
We see your old footprints going away across
The great Republic, Frost, up memorized slopes,
Down hills floating by heart on the bulldozed land.

Poem of Night

1

I move my hand over
Slopes, falls, lumps of sight,
Lashes barely able to be touched,
Lips that give way so easily
It's a shock to feel under them
The indifferent smile of bones.

Muffled a little, barely cloaked,
Zygoma, maxillary, turbinate.

2

I put my hand
On the side of your face,
You lean your head a little
Into my hand—and so,
I know you're a dormouse
Taken up in winter sleep,
A lonely, stunned weight.

3

A cheekbone,
A curved piece of brow,
A pale eyelid
Float in the dark,
And now I make out
An eye, dark,
Wormed with far-off, unaccountable lights.

4

Hardly touching, I hold
What I can only think of

As some deepest of memories in my arms,
Not mine, but as if the life in me
Were slowly remembering what it is.

You lie here now in your physicalness,
This beautiful degree of reality.

5
And now the day, raft that breaks up, comes on.

I think of a few bones
Floating on a river at night,
The starlight blowing in place on the water,
The river leaning like a wave toward the emptiness.

Middle of the Way

1

I wake in the night,
An old ache in the shoulder blades.
I lie amazed under the trees
That creak a little in the dark,
The giant trees of the world.

I lie on earth the way
Flames lie in the woodpile,
Or as an imprint, in sperm or egg, of what is to be.
I love the earth, and always
In its darknesses I am a stranger.

2

6 A.M. Water frozen again. Melted it and made tea. Ate a raw egg and the last orange. Refreshed by a long sleep. The trail practically indistinguishable under 8" of snow. 9:30 A.M. Snow up to my knees in places. Sweat begins freezing under my shirt when I stop to rest. The woods are filled, anyway, with the windy noise of the first streams. 10:30 A.M. The sun at last. The snow starts to melt off the boughs at once, falling with little ticking sounds. Mist clouds are lying in the valleys. 11:45 A.M. Slow, glittering breakers roll in on the beaches ten miles away, very blue and calm. 12 noon. An inexplicable sense of joy, as if some happy news had been transmitted to me directly, by-passing the brain. 2 P.M. From the top of Gauldy I looked back into Hebo valley. Castle Rock sticks into a cloud. A cool breeze comes up from the valley, it is a fresh, earthly wind and tastes of snow and trees. It is not like those transcendental breezes that make the heart ache. It brings happiness. 2:30 P.M. Lost the trail. A woodpecker watches me wade about through the snow trying to locate it. The sun has gone back of the trees. 3:10 P.M. Still hunting for the trail. Getting cold. From an elevation I have an open view to the SE, a world of timberless, white hills, rolling, weirdly wrinkled. Above them a pale half moon. 3:45 P.M. Going on by map and compass. A minute ago a deer fled touching down every fifteen feet or so. 7:30 P.M. Made camp near

the head of Alder Creek. Trampled a bed into the snow and filled it with boughs. Concocted a little fire in the darkness. Ate pork and beans. A slug or two of whiskey burnt my throat. The night very clear. Very cold. That half moon is up there and a lot of stars have come out among the treetops. The fire has fallen to coals.

3

The coals go out,
The last smoke wavers up
Losing itself in the stars.
This is my first night to lie
In the uncreating dark.

In the human heart
There sleeps a green worm
That has spun the heart about itself,
And that shall dream itself black wings
One day to break free into the black sky.

I leave my eyes open,
I lie here and forget our life,
All I see is that we float out
Into the emptiness, among the great stars,
On this little vessel without lights.

I know that I love the day,
The sun on the mountain, the Pacific
Shiny and accomplishing itself in breakers,
But I know I live half alive in the world,
Half my life belongs to the wild darkness.

Ruins Under the Stars

1

All day under acrobat
Swallows I have sat, beside ruins
Of a plank house sunk up to its windows
In burdock and raspberry cane,
The roof dropped, the foundation broken in,
Nothing left perfect but the axe-marks on the beams.

A paper in a cupboard talks about "Mugwumps,"
In a V-letter a farmboy has "tasted battle . . ."
The apples are pure acid on the tangle of boughs,
The pasture has gone to popple and bush.
Here on this perch of ruins
I listen for the crunch of the porcupines.

2

Overhead the skull-hill rises
Crossed on top by the stunted apple,
Infinitely beyond it, older than love or guilt,
Wait the stars ready to jump and sprinkle out of space.

Every night under those thousand lights
An owl dies, a snake sloughs its skin,
A man in a dark pasture
Feels a homesickness he does not understand.

3

Sometimes I see them,
The south-going Canada geese,
At evening, coming down
In pink light, over the pond, in great,
Loose, always-dissolving V's—
I go out into the field to hear

The cold, lonely yelping
Of their tranced bodies in the sky.

4

This morning I watched
Milton Norway's sky-blue Ford
Dragging its ass down the dirt road
On the other side of the valley.

Later, off in the woods,
A chainsaw was agonizing across the top of some stump.
A while ago the tracks of a little, snowy,
SAC bomber crawled across heaven.

What of that hairstreak
That was flopping and batting about
Deep in the goldenrod—
Did she not know, either, where she was going?

5

The bats come spelling the swallows.
In the smoking heap of old antiques
The porcupine-crackle starts up again,
The bone-saw, the ur-music of our sphere,
And up there the stars rustling and whispering.

Flower Herding on Mount Monadnock

1

I can support it no longer.
Laughing ruefully at myself
For all I claim to have suffered
I get up. Damned nightmarer!

It is New Hampshire out here,
It is nearly the dawn.
The song of the whippoorwill stops
And the dimension of depth seizes everything.

2

The whistlings of a peabody bird go overhead
Like a needle pushed five times through the air,
They enter the leaves, and come out little changed.

The air is so still
That as they go off through the trees
The love songs of birds do not get any fainter.

3

The last memory I have
Is of a flower that cannot be touched,

Through the bloom of which, all day,
Fly crazed, missing bees.

4

As I climb sweat gets up my nostrils,
For an instant I think I am at the sea,

One summer off Cap Ferrat we watched a black seagull
Straining for the dawn, we stood in the surf,

Grasshoppers splash up where I step,
The mountain laurel crashes at my thighs.

5

There is something joyous in the elegies
Of birds. They seem
Caught up in a formal delight,
Though the mourning dove whistles of despair.

But at last in the thousand elegies
The dead rise in our hearts,
On the brink of our happiness we stop
Like someone on a drunk starting to weep.

6

I kneel at a pool,
I look through my face
At the bacteria I think
I see crawling through the moss.

My face sees me,
The water stirs, the face,
Looking preoccupied,
Gets knocked from its bones.

7

I weighed eleven pounds
At birth, having stayed on
Two extra weeks in the womb.
Tempted by room and fresh air
I came out big as a policeman,
Blue-faced, with narrow red eyes.
It was eight days before the doctor
Would scare my mother with me.

Turning and craning in the vines
I can make out through the leaves
The old, shimmering nothingness, the sky.

8

Green, scaly moosewoods ascend,
Tenants of the shaken paradise,

At every wind last night's rain
Comes splattering from the leaves,

It drops in flurries and lies there,
The footsteps of some running start.

9

From a rock
A waterfall,
A single trickle like a strand of wire,
Breaks into beads halfway down.

I know
The birds fly off
But the hug of the earth wraps
With moss their graves and the giant boulders.

10

In the forest I discover a flower.

The invisible life of the thing
Goes up in flames that are invisible,
Like cellophane burning in the sunlight.

It burns up. Its drift is to be nothing.

In its covertness it has a way
Of uttering itself in place of itself,
Its blossoms claim to float in the Empyrean,

A wrathful presence on the blur of the ground.

The appeal to heaven breaks off.
The petals begin to fall, in self-forgiveness.
It is a flower. On this mountainside it is dying.

Body Rags

1968

Another Night in the Ruins

1

In the evening
haze darkening on the hills,
purple of the eternal,
a last bird crosses over,
'*flop flop*,' adoring
only the instant.

2

Nine years ago,
in a plane that rumbled all night
above the Atlantic,
I could see, lit up
by lightning bolts jumping out of it,
a thunderhead formed like the face
of my brother, looking bitterly down
on blue,
lightning-flashed moments of the Atlantic.

3

He used to tell me,
"What good is the day?
On some hill of despair
the bonfire
you kindle can light the great sky—
though it's true, of course, to make it burn
you have to throw yourself in . . ."

4

Wind tears itself hollow
in the eaves of these ruins, ghost-flute
of snowdrifts

that build out there in the dark:
upside-down ravines
into which night sweeps
our cast wings, our ink-spattered feathers.

5

I listen.
I hear nothing. Only
the cow, the cow of such
hollowness, mooing
down the bones.

6

Is that a
rooster? He
thrashes in the snow
for a grain. Finds
it. Rips
it into
flames. Flaps. Crows.
Flames
bursting out of his brow.

7

How many nights must it take
one such as me to learn
that we aren't, after all, made
from that bird that flies out of its ashes,
that for us
as we go up in flames, our one work
is
to open ourselves, to *be*
the flames?

Vapor Trail Reflected in the Frog Pond

1

The old watch: their
thick eyes
puff and foreclose by the moon. The young, heads
trailed by the beginnings of necks,
shiver,
in the guarantee they shall be bodies.

In the frog pond
the vapor trail of a SAC bomber creeps,

I hear its drone, drifting, high up
in immaculate ozone.

2

And I hear,
coming over the hills, America singing,
her varied carols I hear:
crack of deputies' rifles practicing their aim on stray dogs at night,
sput of cattleprod,
TV going on about the smells of the human body,
curses of the soldier as he poisons, burns, grinds, and stabs
the rice of the world,
with open mouth, crying strong, hysterical curses.

3

And by paddies in Asia
bones
wearing a few shadows
walk down a dirt road, smashed
bloodsuckers on their heel, knowing
flesh thrown down in the sunshine
dogs shall eat

and flesh flung into the air
shall be seized by birds,
shoulder blades smooth, unmarked by old feather-holes,
hands rivered
by blue, erratic wanderings of the blood,
eyes crinkled shut at almost seeing
the drifting sun that gives us our lives.

The Burn

Twelve years ago I came here
to stray across the burnt land,
I had only begun to know
the kind of pain others endure.
On the dirt road winding
beside the Kilchis River
down to the sea, saplings
on all the hills, I go deep
into the first forest of Douglas firs
shimmering out of prehistory,
a strange shine up where the tops
shut out the sky, whose roots
feed in the waters of the rainbow trout.
And here, at my feet, in the grain
of a burnt log opened by a riverfall,
the swirls of the creation. At the
San Francisco airport, Charlotte,
where yesterday my arms
died around you like old snakeskins, puffed
needletracks on your arms
marked how the veins wander.
I see you walking like a somnambulist
through a poppy field, blind
as myself on this dirt road, tiny
flowers brightening about you,
the skills of fire, of fanning
the blossoms until they flare and die,
perfected; only the power to nurture
and prolong, only this love,
impossible. The mouth of the river.
On these beaches
the sea throws itself down, in flames.

The Fly

The fly
I've just brushed
off my face keeps buzzing
about me, flesh-
eater
starved for the soul.

One day I may learn to suffer
his mizzling, sporadic stroll over eyelid or cheek,
even hear my own notes
in his burnt song.

The bee is the fleur-de-lys in the flesh.
She has a tuft of the sun on her back.
She brings sexual love to the narcissus flower.
She sings of fulfillment only
and stings and dies.
And everything she touches
is opening, opening.

And yet we say our last goodbye
to the fly last,
the flesh-fly last,
the absolute last,
the naked dirty reality of him last.

The Correspondence School Instructor Says Goodbye to His Poetry Students

Goodbye, lady in Bangor, who sent me
snapshots of yourself, after definitely hinting
you were beautiful; goodbye,
Miami Beach urologist, who enclosed plain
brown envelopes for the return of your *very*
"Clinical Sonnets"; goodbye, manufacturer
of brassieres on the Coast, whose eclogues
give the fullest treatment in literature yet
to the sagging breast motif; goodbye, you in San Quentin,
who wrote, "Being German my hero is Hitler,"
instead of "Sincerely yours," at the end of long,
neat-scripted letters extolling the Pre-Raphaelites:

I swear to you, it was just my way
of cheering myself up, as I licked
the stamped, self-addressed envelopes,
the game I had of trying to guess
which one of you, this time,
had poisoned his glue. I did care.
I did read each poem entire.
I did say what I thought
in the mildest words I knew. And now,
in this poem, or chopped prose, no better,
I realize, than those troubled lines
I kept sending back to you,
I have to say I am relieved it is over:
at the end I could feel only pity
for that urge toward more life
your poems kept smothering in words, the smell
of which, days later, tingled
in your nostrils as new, God-given impulses
to write.

Goodbye,
you who are, for me, the postmarks again
of imaginary towns—Xenia, Burnt Cabins, Hornell—
their solitude given away in poems, only their loneliness kept.

How Many Nights

How many nights
have I lain in terror,
O Creator Spirit, maker of night and day,

only to walk out
the next morning over the frozen world
hearing under the creaking of snow
faint, peaceful breaths . . .
snake,
bear, earthworm, ant . . .

and above me
a wild crow crying 'yaw yaw yaw'
from a branch nothing cried from ever in my life.

The Porcupine

1

Fatted
on herbs, swollen on crabapples,
puffed up on bast and phloem, ballooned
on willow flowers, poplar catkins, first
leafs of aspen and larch,
the porcupine
drags and bounces his last meal through ice,
mud, roses and goldenrod, into the stubbly high fields.

2

In character
he resembles us in seven ways:
he puts his mark on outhouses,
he alchemizes by moonlight,
he shits on the run,
he uses his tail for climbing,
he chuckles softly to himself when scared,
he's overcrowded if there's more than one of him per five acres,
his eyes have their own inner redness.

3

Digger of
goings across floors, of hesitations
at thresholds, of
handprints of dread
at doorpost or window jamb, he would
gouge the world
empty of us, hack and crater
it
until it is nothing, if that
could rid it of all our sweat and pathos.

Adorer of ax
handles aflow with grain, of arms
of Morris chairs, of hand
crafted objects
steeped in the juice of fingertips,
of surfaces wetted down
with fist grease and elbow oil,
of clothespins that have
grabbed our body rags by underarm and crotch . . .

Unimpressed—bored—
by the whirl of the stars, by *these*
he's astonished, ultra-
Rilkean angel!

for whom the true
portion of the sweetness of earth
is one of those bottom-heavy, glittering, saccadic
bits
of salt water that splash down
the haunted ravines of a human face.

4
A farmer shot a porcupine three times
as it dozed on a tree limb. On
the way down it tore open its belly
on a broken
branch, hooked its gut,
and went on falling. On the ground
it sprang to its feet
and paying out gut heaved
and spartled through a hundred feet of goldenrod
before
the abrupt emptiness.

5
The Avesta
puts porcupine killers
into hell for nine generations, sentencing them

to gnaw out
each other's hearts for the
salts of desire.

I roll
this way and that in the great bed, under
the quilt
that mimics this country of broken farms and woods,
the fatty sheath of the man
melting off,
the self-stabbing coil
of bristles reversing, blossoming outward—
a red-eyed, hard-toothed, arrow-stuck urchin
tossing up mattress feathers,
pricking the
woman beside me until she cries.

6

In my time I have
crouched, quills erected,
Saint
Sebastian of the
scared heart, and been
beat dead with a locust club
on the bare snout.
And fallen from high places
I have fled, have
jogged
over fields of goldenrod,
terrified, seeking home,
and among flowers
I have come to myself empty, the rope
strung out behind me
in the fall sun
suddenly glorified with all my blood.

7

And tonight I think I prowl broken
skulled or vacant as a

sucked egg in the wintry meadow, softly chuckling, blank
template of myself, dragging
a starved belly through the lichflowered acres,
where burdock looses its arks of seed
and thistle holds up its lost blooms
and rosebushes in the wind scrape their dead limbs
for the forced-fire
of roses.

The Bear

In late winter
I sometimes glimpse bits of steam
coming up from
some fault in the old snow
and bend close and see it is lung-colored
and put down my nose
and know
the chilly, enduring odor of bear.

2

I take a wolf's rib and whittle
it sharp at both ends
and coil it up
and freeze it in blubber and place it out
on the fairway of the bears.

And when it has vanished
I move out on the bear tracks,
roaming in circles
until I come to the first, tentative, dark
splash on the earth.

And I set out
running, following the splashes
of blood wandering over the world.
At the cut, gashed resting places
I stop and rest,
at the crawl-marks
where he lay out on his belly
to overpass some stretch of bauchy ice
I lie out
dragging myself forward with bear-knives in my fists.

3

On the third day I begin to starve,
at nightfall I bend down as I knew I would
at a turd sopped in blood,
and hesitate, and pick it up,
and thrust it in my mouth, and gnash it down,
and rise
and go on running.

4

On the seventh day,
living by now on bear blood alone,
I can see his upturned carcass far out ahead, a scraggled,
steamy hulk,
the heavy fur riffling in the wind.

I come up to him
and stare at the narrow-spaced, petty eyes,
the dismayed
face laid back on the shoulder, the nostrils
flared, catching
perhaps the first taint of me as he
died.

I hack
a ravine in his thigh, and eat and drink,
and tear him down his whole length
and open him and climb in
and close him up after me, against the wind,
and sleep.

5

And dream
of lumbering flatfooted
over the tundra,
stabbed twice from within,
splattering a trail behind me,
splattering it out no matter which way I lurch,
no matter which parabola of bear-transcendence,

which dance of solitude I attempt,
which gravity-clutched leap,
which trudge, which groan.

6

Until one day I totter and fall—
fall on this
stomach that has tried so hard to keep up,
to digest the blood as it leaked in,
to break up
and digest the bone itself: and now the breeze
blows over me, blows off
the hideous belches of ill-digested bear blood
and rotted stomach
and the ordinary, wretched odor of bear,

blows across
my sore, lolled tongue a song
or screech, until I think I must rise up
and dance. And I lie still.

7

I awaken I think. Marshlights
reappear, geese
come trailing again up the flyway.
In her ravine under old snow the dam-bear
lies, licking
lumps of smeared fur
and drizzly eyes into shapes
with her tongue. And one
hairy-soled trudge stuck out before me,
the next groaned out,
the next,
the next,
the rest of my days I spend
wandering: wondering
what, anyway,
was that sticky infusion, that rank flavor of blood, that poetry, by which
    I lived?

FROM

The Book of Nightmares

1971

NOTE:

The Book of Nightmares,
a poem in ten parts, is
represented here by
parts I, II, VI, VII,
and X.

Under the Maud Moon

1

On the path,
by this wet site
of old fires—
black ashes, black stones, where tramps
must have squatted down,
gnawing on stream water,
unhouseling themselves on cursed bread,
failing to get warm at a twigfire—

I stop,
gather wet wood,
cut dry shavings, and for her,
whose face
I held in my hands
a few hours, whom I gave back
only to keep holding the space where she was,

I light
a small fire in the rain.

The black
wood reddens, the deathwatches inside
begin running out of time, I can see
the dead, crossed limbs
longing again for the universe, I can hear
in the wet wood the snap
and re-snap of the same embrace being torn.

The raindrops trying
to put the fire out
fall into it and are
changed: the oath broken,
the oath sworn between earth and water, flesh and spirit, broken,
to be sworn again,

over and over, in the clouds, and broken again,
over and over, on earth.

2

I sit awhile
by the fire, in the rain, speak
a few words into its warmth—
stone saint smooth stone—and murmur
one of the songs I used to croak
to my daughter, in her nightmares.

Somewhere out ahead of me
a black bear sits alone
on his hillside, nodding from side
to side. He sniffs
the blossom-smells, the rained earth,
finally he gets up,
eats a few flowers, trudges away,
all his fur glistening
in the rain.

The singed grease streams
out of the words, the one
held note
remains—a love-note
twisting under my tongue, like the coyote's bark,
curving off, into a
howl.

3

A round-
cheeked girlchild comes awake
in her crib. The green
swaddlings tear open,
a filament or vestment
tears, the blue
flower opens.

And she who is born,
she who sings and cries,
she who begins the passage, her hair
sprouting out,
her gums budding for her first spring on earth,
the mist still clinging about
her face, puts
her hand
into her mother's mouth, to take hold of
her song.

4

It is all over,
little one, the flipping
and overleaping, the watery
somersaulting alone in the oneness
under the hill, under
the old, lonely bellybutton
pushing forth again
in remembrance,
the drifting there furled in the dark,
pressing a knee or elbow
along a slippery wall, sculpting
the world with each thrash—the stream
of omphalos blood humming all about you.

5

Her head
enters the headhold
that starts sucking her forth: existence
closes down all over her, draws her
into the shuddering
grip of departure, the slow,
agonized clenches making
the last molds of her life in the dark.

6

The black eye
opens, the pupil
droozed with black hairs
stops, the chakra
on top of the brain throbs a long moment in world light,

and she skids out on her face into light,
this peck
of stunned flesh
clotted with celestial cheesiness, glowing
with the astral violet
of the underlife. As they cut

her tie to the darkness
she dies
a moment, turns blue as a coal,
the limbs shaking
as the memories rush out of them. When

they hang her up
by the feet, she sucks
air, screams
her first song—and turns rose,
the slow,
beating, featherless arms
already clutching at the emptiness.

7

When it was cold
on our hillside, and you cried
in the crib rocking
through the darkness, on wood
knifed down to the curve of the smile, a sadness
stranger than ours, all of it
turned back toward the other world,

I used to come to you
and sit by you
and sing to you. You did not know,

and yet you will remember,
in the silent zones
of the brain, a specter, descendant
of the ghostly forefathers, singing
to you in the nighttime—
not the songs
of light said to wave
through the bright hair of angels,
but a blacker
rasping flowering on that tongue.

For when the Maud moon
glimmered in those first nights,
and the Archer lay
sucking the icy biestings of the cosmos
in his crib of stars,

I had crept down
to riverbanks, their long rustle
of being and perishing, down to marshes
where the earth oozes up
in cold streaks, touching the world
with the underglimmer
of the beginning,
and there learned my only song.

And in the days
when you find yourself orphaned,
emptied
of wind-singing, of light,
the pieces of cursed bread on your tongue,

may there come back to you
a voice,
spectral, calling you
sister!
from everything that dies.

And then
you shall open
this book, even if it is the book of nightmares.

The Hen Flower

1

Sprawled
on our faces in the spring
nights, teeth
biting down on hen feathers, bits of the hen
still stuck in the crevices — if only
we could let ourselves go
like her, throw ourselves
on the mercy of darkness, like the hen,

tuck our head
under a wing, hold ourselves still
a few moments, as she
falls out into her little trance in the witchgrass,
or turn over
and be stroked with a finger
down the throat feathers,
down the throat knuckles,
down over the hum
of the wishbone tuning its high D in thin blood,
down over
the breastbone risen up
out of breast flesh, until the fatted thing
woozes off, head
thrown back
on the chopping block, longing only
to die.

2

When the axe-
scented breeze flourishes
about her, her cheeks crush in,
her comb
grays, the gizzard
that turns the thousand acidic millstones of her fate

convulses: ready or not
the next egg, bobbling
its globe of golden earth,
skids forth, ridding her even
of the life to come.

3

Almost high
on subsided gravity, I remain afoot,
a hen flower
dangling from a hand,
wing
of my wing,
of my bones and veins,
of my flesh
hairs lifting all over me in the first ghostly breeze
after death,

wing
made only to fly—unable
to write out the sorrows of being unable
to hold another in one's arms—and unable
to fly,
and waiting, therefore,
for the sweet, eventual blaze in the genes,
that one day, according to gospel, shall carry it back
into pink skies, where geese
cross at twilight, honking
in tongues.

4

I have glimpsed
by corpse-light, in the opened cadaver
of hen, the mass of tiny,
unborn eggs, each getting
tinier and yellower as it reaches back toward
the icy pulp
of what is, I have felt the zero
freeze itself around the finger dipped slowly in.

5

When the Northern Lights
were opening across the black sky and vanishing,
lighting themselves up
so completely they were vanishing,
I put to my eye the lucent
section of the spealbone of a ram—

I thought suddenly
I could read the cosmos spelling itself,
the huge broken letters
shuddering across the black sky and vanishing,

and in a moment,
in the twinkling of an eye, it came to me
the mockingbird would sing all her nights the cry of the rifle,
the tree would hold the bones of the sniper who dared not climb down,
the rose would bloom no one would see it,
the chameleon longing to be changed would remain the color of blood.

And I went up
to the henhouse, and took up
the hen killed by weasels, and lugged
the sucked
carcass into first light. And when I hoisted
her up among the young pines, a last
rubbery egg slipping out as I flung her high, didn't it happen
the dead
wings creaked open as she soared
across the arms of the Bear?

6

Sprawled face down, waiting
for the rooster to groan out
it is the empty morning, as he groaned out thrice
for the disciple
of stone,
he who crushed with his heel the brain out of the snake,

I remember long ago I sowed
my own first milk
tooth under hen feathers, I planted under hen feathers
the hook
of the wishbone,
which had broken itself toward me.

For the future.

It has come to this.

7

Listen, Kinnell,
dumped alive
and dying into the old sway bed,
a layer of crushed feathers all that there is
between you
and the long shaft of darkness shaped as you,
let go.

Even this haunted room
all its materials photographed with tragedy,
even the tiny crucifix drifting face down at the center of the earth,
even these feathers freed from their wings forever
are afraid.

The Dead Shall Be Raised Incorruptible

1

A piece of flesh gives off
smoke in the field—

caput mortuum,
orts,
pelf,
nast,
fenks,
sordes,
gurry dumped from hospital trashcans.

Lieutenant!
This corpse will not stop burning!

2

"That you Captain? Sure,
sure I remember—I still hear you
lecturing at me on the intercom, *Keep your guns up, Burnsie!*
and then screaming, *Stop shooting, for crissake, Burnsie,*
those are friendlies! But crissake, Captain,
I'd already started, burst
after burst, little black pajamas jumping
and falling . . . and remember that pilot
who'd bailed out over the North,
how I shredded him down to a bunch of guts on his strings?
one of his slant eyes, a piece
of his smile, sail past me
every night right after the sleeping pill . . .

"It was only
that I loved the *sound*
of them, I guess I just loved
the *feel* of them sparkin' off my hands . . ."

3

On the television screen:

Do you have a body that sweats?
Sweat that has odor?
False teeth dropping into your breakfast?
Case of the dread?
Headache so steady it may outlive you?
Armpits sprouting hair?
Piles so huge you hardly need a chair to sit at a table?

We shall not all sleep, but we shall be changed . . .

4

In the Twentieth Century of my trespass on earth,
having exterminated all I could of heathens,
heretics, Jews, Moslems, witches, mystical seekers,
Asians, black men, and white Christian brothers,
every one of them for his own good,

a continent of red men for living in community
and having spiritual relations with the land,
one billion species of animals for being sub-human,
and ready to take on the bloodthirsty creatures from the other planets,
I, white Christian man, groan out this testament of my last will.

I give my blood fifty parts polystyrene,
twenty-five parts benzene, twenty-five parts good old gasoline,
to the last bomber pilot aloft, that there shall be one acre
in the dull world where the kissing flower may bloom,
which kisses you so long your bones explode under its lips.

My tongue goes to the Secretary of the Dead
to tell the corpses, "I'm sorry, fellows,
the killing was just one of those things
difficult to pre-visualize—like a cow,
say, getting blown up by lightning."

My stomach, which has digested
four hundred treaties giving the Indians
the right to their land, I give to the Indians,
as well as my lungs full of tumors from faithfully
smoking the peace pipe before every massacre.

My soul I leave to the bee
that he may sting it and die, my brain
to the fly, his back the hysterical color of slime,
that he may eat it and die, my flesh to the advertising man,
the anti-prostitute, who loathes human flesh for money.

I assign my crooked backbone
to the dice maker, to chop up into dice,
for casting lots as to who shall see his own blood
on his shirt front and who his brother's,
for the race isn't to the swift but to the crooked.

To the last person surviving on earth
I give my eyelids worn out by fear, to wear
in the long nights of radiation and silence,
so that the eyes can't close, for regret
is like tears seeping through closed eyelids.

I give the emptiness my hand: the pinkie picks no more,
slag clings to the black stick of the ring finger,
a bit of flame jets from the tip of the fuck-you finger,
the first finger accuses the heart, which has vanished,
on the thumb stump wisps of smoke ask a ride into the emptiness.

In the Twentieth Century of my nightmare
on earth, I swear on my chromium testicles
to this testament
and last will
of my iron will, my fear of love, my itch for money, and my madness.

5
In the ditch
snakes crawl cool paths

over the rotted thigh, the toe bones
twitch in the smell of burnt rubber,
the belly
opens like a deadly nightflower,
the tongue has evaporated,
the nostril
hairs sprinkle themselves with yellowish-white dust,
the five flames at the end
of each hand go out, a mosquito
sips a last meal from this plate of serenity.

And the fly,
the last nightmare, hatches himself.

6

I ran
my neck broken I ran
holding my head up with both hands I ran
thinking the flames
the flames may burn the oboe
but listen buddy boy they can't touch the notes.

7

A few bones
lie about in the smoke of bones.

Effigies pressed into grass,
mummy windings,
desquamations,
union suits on racks in thrift shops
sags incinerated mattresses gave back to the world,
memories left in mirrors on bedroom ceilings,
angel's wings
flagged down into the snows of yesteryear,

kneel
on the scorched earth

in the shapes of men and animals:
do not let this last hour pass,
do not remove this last, poisoned cup from our lips.

And a wind holding
the cries of love-making from our nights and days
moves among the stones, hunting
for two twined skeletons to blow its last cry across.

Lieutenant!
This corpse will not stop burning!

Little Sleep's-Head Sprouting Hair in the Moonlight

1

You cry, waking from a nightmare.

When I sleepwalk
into your room, and pick you up,
and hold you up in the moonlight, you cling to me
hard,
as if clinging could save us. I think
you think
I will never die, I think I exude
to you the permanence of smoke or stars,
even as
my broken arms heal themselves around you.

2

I have heard you tell
the sun, *don't go down*, I have stood by
as you told the flower, *don't grow old,
don't die*. Little Maud,

I would blow the flame out of your silver cup,
I would suck the rot from your fingernail,
I would brush your sprouting hair of the dying light,
I would scrape the rust off your ivory bones,
I would help death escape through the little ribs of your body,
I would alchemize the ashes of your cradle back into wood,
I would let nothing of you go, ever,

until washerwomen
feel the clothes fall asleep in their hands,
and hens scratch their spell across hatchet blades,
and rats walk away from the cultures of the plague,
and iron twists weapons toward the truth north,
and grease refuses to slide in the machinery of progress,

and men feel as free on earth as fleas on the bodies of men,
and the widow still whispers back and forth with the presence no longer
    beside her in the dark.

And yet perhaps this is the reason you cry,
this the nightmare you wake crying from:
being forever
in the pre-trembling of a house that falls.

3

In a restaurant once, everyone
quietly eating, you clambered up
on my lap: to all
the mouthfuls rising toward
all the mouths, at the top of your voice
you cried
your one word, *caca! caca! caca!*
and each spoonful
stopped, a moment, in midair, in its withering
steam.

Yes,
you cling because
I, like you, only sooner
than you, will go down
the path of vanished alphabets,
the roadlessness
to the other side of the darkness,
your arms
like the shoes left behind,
like the adjectives
in the halting speech of old folks,
which once could call up the lost nouns.

4

And you yourself,
some impossible Tuesday
in the year Two Thousand and Nine, will walk out

among the black stones
of the field, in the rain,

and the stones saying
over their one word, *ci-gît, ci-gît, ci-gît,*

and the raindrops
hitting you on the fontanel
over and over, and you standing there
unable to let them in.

5

If one day it happens
you find yourself with someone you love
in a café at one end
of the Pont Mirabeau, at the zinc bar
where wine finds its shapes in upward opening glasses,

and if you commit then, as we did, the error
of thinking,
one day all this will only be memory,

learn to reach deeper
into the sorrows
to come—to touch
the almost imaginary bones
under the face, to hear under the laughter
the wind crying across the black stones. Kiss
the mouth
that tells you, *here,*
here is the world. This mouth. This laughter. These temple bones.

The still undanced cadence of vanishing.

6

In the light the moon
sends back, I can see in your eyes

the hand that waved once
in my father's eyes, a tiny kite
wobbling far up in the twilight of his last look:

and the angel
of all mortal things lets go the string.

7

Back you go, into your crib.

The last blackbird lights up his gold wings: *farewell.*
Your eyes close inside your head,
in sleep. Already
in your dreams the hours begin to sing.

Little sleep's-head sprouting hair in the moonlight,
when I come back
we will go out together,
we will walk out together among
the ten thousand things,
each scratched in time with such knowledge, *the wages*
of dying is love.

Lastness

1

The skinny waterfalls, footpaths
wandering out of heaven, strike
the cliffside, leap, and shudder off.

Somewhere behind me
a small fire goes on flaring in the rain, in the desolate ashes.
No matter, now, whom it was built for,
it keeps its flames,
it warms
everyone who might stray into its radiance,
a tree, a lost animal, the stones,

because in the dying world it was set burning.

2

A black bear sits alone
in the twilight, nodding from side
to side, turning slowly around and around
on himself, scuffing the four-footed
circle into the earth. He sniffs the sweat
in the breeze, he understands
a creature, a death-creature,
watches from the fringe of the trees,
finally he understands
I am no longer here, he himself
from the fringe of the trees watches
a black bear
get up, eat a few flowers, trudge away,
all his fur glistening
in the rain.

And what glistening! Sancho Fergus,
my boychild, had such great shoulders,

when he was born his head
came out, the rest of him stuck. And he opened
his eyes: his head out there all alone
in the room, he squinted with pained,
barely unglued eyes at the ninth-month's
blood splashing beneath him
on the floor. And almost
smiled, I thought, almost forgave it all in advance.

When he came wholly forth
I took him up in my hands and bent
over and smelled
the black, glistening fur
of his head, as empty space
must have bent
over the newborn planet
and smelled the grasslands and the ferns.

3

Walking toward the cliff overhanging
the river, I call out to the stone,
and the stone
calls back, its voice searching among the rubble
for my ears.

Stop.
As you approach an echoing
cliffside, you sense the line
where the voice calling from stone
no longer answers,
turns into stone, and nothing comes back.

Here, between answer
and nothing, I stand, in the old shoes
flowed over by rainbows of hen-oil,
each shoe holding the bones
that ripple together in the communion
of the step
and that open out

in front into toes, the whole foot trying
to dissolve into the future.

A clatter of elk hooves.
Has the top sphere
emptied itself? Is it true
the earth is all there is, and the earth does not last?

On the river the world floats by holding one corpse.

Stop.
Stop here.
Living brings you to death, there is no other road.

4

This is the tenth poem
and it is the last. It is right
at the last, that one
and zero
walk off together,
walk off the end of these pages together,
one creature
walking away side by side with the emptiness.

Lastness
is brightness. It is the brightness
gathered up of all that went before. It lasts.
And when it does end
there is nothing, nothing
left,

in the rust of old cars,
in the hole torn open in the body of the Archer,
in river-mist smelling of the weariness of stones,
the dead lie,
empty, filled, at the beginning,

and the first
voice comes craving again out of their mouths.

5

That Bach concert I went to so long ago—
the chandeliered room
of ladies and gentlemen who would never die . . .
the voices go out,
the room becomes hushed,
the violinist
puts the irreversible sorrow of his face
into the opened palm
of the wood, the music begins:

a shower of rosin,
the bow-hairs listening down all their length
to the wail,
the sexual wail
of the back-alleys and blood strings we have lived
still crying,
still singing, from the sliced intestine
of cat.

6

This poem
if we shall call it that,
or concert of one
divided among himself,
this earthward gesture
of the sky-diver, the worms
on his back still spinning forth
and already gnawing away
the silks of his loves, who could have saved him,
this free floating of one
opening his arms into the attitude
of flight, as he obeys the necessity and falls . . .

7

Sancho Fergus! Don't cry!

Or else, cry.

On the body,
on the yellowed flesh, when it is
laid out, see if you can find
the one flea that is laughing.

Mortal Acts,
Mortal Words

1980

Fergus Falling

He climbed to the top
of one of those million white pines
set out across the emptying pastures
of the fifties—some program to enrich the rich
and rebuke the forefathers
who cleared it all once with ox and axe—
climbed to the top, probably to get out
of the shadow
not of those forefathers but of this father,
and saw for the first time,
down in its valley, Bruce Pond, giving off
its little steam in the afternoon,

pond where Clarence Akley came on Sunday mornings to cut down
    the cedars around the shore, I'd sometimes hear the slow
    spondees of his work, he's gone,
where Milton Norway came up behind me while I was fishing and
    stood awhile before I knew he was there, he's the one who put
    the cedar shingles on the house, some have curled or split, a
    few have blown off, he's gone,
where Gus Newland logged in the cold snap of '58, the only man
    willing to go into those woods that never got warmer than ten
    below, he's gone,
pond where two wards of the state wandered on Halloween, the
    National Guard searched for them in November, in vain, the
    next fall a hunter found their skeletons huddled together, in
    vain, they're gone,
pond where an old fisherman in a rowboat sits, drowning hooked
    worms, when he goes he's replaced and he's never gone,

and when Fergus
saw the pond for the first time
in the clear evening, saw its oldness down there
in its old place in the valley, he became heavier suddenly
in his bones

the way fledglings do just before they fly,
and the soft pine cracked . . .

I would not have heard his cry
if my electric saw had been working,
its carbide teeth speeding through the bland spruce of our time, or
    scorching
black arcs into some scavenged hemlock plank,
like dark circles under eyes
when the brain thinks too close to the skin,
but I was sawing by hand and I heard that cry
as though he were attacked; we ran out,
when we bent over him he said, "Galway, Inés, I saw a pond!"
His face went gray, his eyes fluttered closed a frightening moment . . .

Yes—a pond
that lets off its mist
on clear afternoons of August, in that valley
to which many have come, for their reasons,
from which many have gone, a few for their reasons, most not,
where even now an old fisherman only the pinetops can see
sits in the dry gray wood of his rowboat, waiting for pickerel.

After Making Love We Hear Footsteps

For I can snore like a bullhorn
or play loud music
or sit up talking with any reasonably sober Irishman
and Fergus will only sink deeper
into his dreamless sleep, which goes by all in one flash,
but let there be that heavy breathing
or a stifled come-cry anywhere in the house
and he will wrench himself awake
and make for it on the run—as now, we lie together,
after making love, quiet, touching along the length of our bodies,
familiar touch of the long-married,
and he appears—in his baseball pajamas, it happens,
the neck opening so small he has to screw them on—
and flops down between us and hugs us and snuggles himself to sleep,
his face gleaming with satisfaction at being this very child.

In the half darkness we look at each other
and smile
and touch arms across this little, startlingly muscled body—
this one whom habit of memory propels to the ground of his making,
sleeper only the mortal sounds can sing awake,
this blessing love gives again into our arms.

Saint Francis and the Sow

The bud
stands for all things,
even for those things that don't flower,
for everything flowers, from within, of self-blessing;
though sometimes it is necessary
to reteach a thing its loveliness,
to put a hand on its brow
of the flower
and retell it in words and in touch
it is lovely
until it flowers again from within, of self-blessing;
as Saint Francis
put his hand on the creased forehead
of the sow, and told her in words and in touch
blessings of earth on the sow, and the sow
began remembering all down her thick length,
from the earthen snout all the way
through the fodder and slops to the spiritual curl of the tail,
from the hard spininess spiked out from the spine
down through the great broken heart
to the sheer blue milken dreaminess spurting and shuddering
from the fourteen teats into the fourteen mouths sucking and blowing
        beneath them:
the long, perfect loveliness of sow.

Wait

Wait, for now.
Distrust everything if you have to.
But trust the hours. Haven't they
carried you everywhere, up to now?
Personal events will become interesting again.
Hair will become interesting.
Pain will become interesting.
Buds that open out of season will become interesting.
Second-hand gloves will become lovely again;
their memories are what give them
the need for other hands. The desolation
of lovers is the same: that enormous emptiness
carved out of such tiny beings as we are
asks to be filled; the need
for the new love *is* faithfulness to the old.

Wait.
Don't go too early.
You're tired. But everyone's tired.
But no one is tired enough.
Only wait a little and listen:
music of hair,
music of pain,
music of looms weaving our loves again.
Be there to hear it, it will be the only time,
most of all to hear your whole existence,
rehearsed by the sorrows, play itself into total exhaustion.

Daybreak

On the tidal mud, just before sunset,
dozens of starfishes
were creeping. It was
as though the mud were a sky
and enormous, imperfect stars
moved across it as slowly
as the actual stars cross heaven.
All at once they stopped,
and, as if they had simply
increased their receptivity
to gravity, they sank down
into the mud, faded down
into it and lay still, and by the time
pink of sunset broke across them
they were as invisible
as the true stars at daybreak.

Blackberry Eating

I love to go out in late September
among the fat, overripe, icy, black blackberries
to eat blackberries for breakfast,
the stalks very prickly, a penalty
they earn for knowing the black art
of blackberry making; and as I stand among them
lifting the stalks to my mouth, the ripest berries
fall almost unbidden to my tongue,
as words sometimes do, certain peculiar words
like *strengths* or *squinched* or *broughamed*,
many-lettered, one-syllabled lumps,
which I squeeze, squinch open, and splurge well
in the silent, startled, icy, black language
of blackberry eating in late September.

Kissing the Toad

Somewhere this dusk
a girl puckers her mouth
and considers kissing
the toad a boy has plucked
from the cornfield and hands
her with both hands,
rough and lichenous
but for the immense ivory belly,
like those old fat cats
sprawling on Mediterranean beaches,
with popped eyes,
it watches the girl who might kiss it,
pisses, quakes, tries
to make its smile wider:
to love on, oh yes, to love on.

On the Tennis Court at Night

We step out on the green rectangle
in moonlight. The lines glow,
which for many have been the only lines
of justice. We remember
the thousand erased trajectories
of that close-contested last set—
blur of volleys, soft arcs of drop shots,
huge ingrown loops of lobs with topspin
that went running away, crosscourts recrossing
down to each sweet (and in exact proportion, bitter)
✪ in Talbert and Olds' *The Game of Doubles in Tennis.*
The breeze has carried them off but we still hear
the mutters, the doublefaulter's groans,
cries of "Deuce!" or "Love two!",
squeak of tennis shoes, grunt of overreaching,
all dozen extant tennis quips—"Just out!"
or, "About right for you?" or, "Want to change partners?"—
and *baaah* of sheep translated very occasionally
into *thonk* of well-hit ball, among the pure
right angles and unhesitating lines
of this arena where every man grows old
pursuing that repertoire of perfect shots,
darkness already in his strokes,
even in death cramps squeezing a tennis ball
for arm strength, to the disgust of the night nurse,
and smiling; and a few hours later found dead—
the smile still in place but the ice bag
left cooling the brow now mysteriously
icing the right elbow—causing
all those bright trophies to slip permanently,
though not in fact much farther, out of reach,
all except for the thick-bottomed young man
about to doublefault in soft metal on the windowsill:
"Runner-Up Men's Class B Consolation Doubles
St. Johnsbury Kiwanis Tennis Tournament 1969" . . .

Clouds come over the moon;
all the lines go out. November last year
in Lyndonville: it is getting dark,
snow starts falling, Zander Rubin wobble-twists
his worst serve out of the black woods behind him,
Tommy Glines lobs into a gust of snow,
Don Bredes smashes at where in theory the ball
could be coming down, the snow blows
and swirls about our legs, darkness flows
across a disappearing patch of green-painted asphalt
in the north country, where four souls,
half-volleying, poaching, missing, grunting,
begging mercy of their bones, hold their ground,
as winter comes on, all the winters to come.

The Last Hiding Places of Snow

1

The burnt tongue
fluttered, "I'm dying . . ."
and then, "Why did . . . ? Why . . . ?"
What earthly knowledge did she still need
just then, when
the tongue failed
or else began speaking in another direction?

Only the struggle for breath
remained: groans made
of all the goodbyes ever spoken
all turned meaningless; surplus world sucked back
into a body laboring to live
as far as it could into death; and past it, if it must.

There is a place in the woods
where one can hear
such sounds: sighs, groans
seeming to come
from the purplish murk of spruce boughs,
from the glimmer-at-night of white birches,
from the last hiding places of snow,

wind,
that's all, driven
across obstructions: every stump
speaks,
the spruce needles play out of it
the sorrows cried into it somewhere else.

Once in a while, passing the place,
I've imagined I heard
my old mother calling, thinking out loud her
feelings toward me, over those many miles
from where her bones lie,

five years
in earth now, with my father's thirty-years' bones.

I used to feel
anointed by what I thought was her love, its light
seeming then like sunlight
falling through broken panes
onto the floor
of a deserted house: we may go, it remains,
telling of goodness of being, of permanence.

So lighted I imagined
I could wander anywhere,
among any foulnesses, any contagions,
I could climb through the entire empty world
and find my way back and learn again to be happy.

But when I stopped and listened,
all I heard was
what may once have been speech
or groans, now shredded down
to a hiss by this valley of needles.

2

I was not at her bedside
that final day, I did not grant her ancient,
huge-knuckled hand
its last wish, I did not let it
let go of the son's hand gradually—and so
hand her, with some steadiness, into the future.

Instead, old age took her
by force, though with the aid
of her old, broken attachments
which had broken
only on this side of death
but kept intact on the other.

I would know myself lucky if my own children
could be at my deathbed, to take

my hand in theirs and with theirs
bless me momentarily back into the world,
with smoothness pressed into roughness,
with folding-light fresh runner hands to runner of wasted breath,
with mortal touch whose mercy two bundled-up figures greeting on a
    freezing morning, each extending the ribboned end of an arm
    and entwining these, squeeze back and forth before walking on,
with memories these hands keep, of strolling down Bethune Street in
    spring, a little creature hanging from each arm by a hand that can
    do no more than press its tiny thumb into the soft beneath my thumb.

But for my own mother I was not there . . .
and at the gates of the world, between
holy ground
and ground of almost all its holiness gone, I loiter
in stupid fantasies I can live that day again.

Why did you come so late?
Why will you go too early?

I know there are regrets
we can never be rid of,
that fade but never leave:
permanent remorse. Knowing this, I know also
I am to draw from that surplus stored up
of tenderness that was hers by right,
which it's possible no one ever gave her,
and give it away, freely.

3

A child, a little girl,
in violet hat, blue scarf, green sweater, yellow skirt, orange socks, red boots,
on a rope swings, swings
in sunlight
over a garden in Ireland, backfalls,
backrises,
forthsinks,
forthsoars, her charmed life holding its breath
innocent of groans, beyond any
future, far past the past: into a pure present.

Now she wears rhythmically into the air of morning
the rainbow's curve, but upside down
so that the angels might see
beloved dross promising heaven:
no matter what fire we invent to destroy us
ours will have been the brightest world ever existing.

Every so often, when I look
at the dark sky, I know she remains
among the old endless blue lightedness
of stars; or finding myself out in a field
in November, when a strange
starry perhaps first snowfall blows
down across the darkening air, lightly,
I know she is there, where snow
falls   flakes   down   fragile   softly
falling until I can't see the earth
any longer, only its shrouded shapes.

Even now, waking sometimes
in some room far from everyone,
I can feel the darkness lightening a little,
and then, because of nothing,
in spite of nothing,
in an imaginary daybreak, I see her,
and for that moment I am still her son
and again in the holy land, and twice in the holy land,
remembered within her, and remembered in the memory
her old body slowly executes into the earth.

Looking at Your Face

Looking at your face
now you have become ready to die
is like kneeling at an old gravestone
on an afternoon without sun, trying to read
the white chiselings of the poem
in the white stone.

Fisherman

for Allen Planz

Solitary man, standing
on the Atlantic, high up on the floodtide
under the moon, hauling at nets
that shudder sideways under the mutilated darkness:
the one you hugged and slept with so often,
who hugged you and slept with you so often,
who has gone away now
into the imaginary moonlight of the greater world,
perhaps looks back at where you stand abandoned
on the floodtide, hauling at nets
and dragging from the darkness
anything, and reaches back
to touch you
and speak to you
from that other relation to which she suddenly acquiesced
     dumbfounded,
but instead only sings
in the sea-birds and breeze you imagine you remember but truly hear.

I don't know how you loved
or what marriage was and wasn't between you—
not even close friends understand very much of that—
but I know ordinary life was hard
and worry joined your brains' faces in pure, baffled lines,
and therefore some part of you will have gone
with her, imprinted now
into that world that she alone doesn't fear,
and that now you will have partly ceased fearing,
and waits there to recognize you into it
after you've lived, lived past the sorrows,
if that happens, after all the time in the world.

52 Oswald Street

for my sisters, Wendy and Jill

Then, when the full moonlight
would touch our blanketed bodies,
we liked to think it filled
us with actual bright matter
drifted down from the regions
of the moon, so that when we woke
we would be changed. Now,
wherever we are on earth,
in loneliness, or loneliness-
easing arms, we three
who have survived the lives
and deaths in the old house
on Oswald Street can almost
feel that full moonlight again,
as someone might almost hear the slow-
given sighs of post-coital bliss
the lover who slipped away could be
breathing this minute in someone
else's arms, and almost taste
the lost fullness and know how
far our hearts have fallen, how
feelings too long attuned
to having don't bear up,
and how for us it turns out
three gravesides are too many
to stand at, or turn from,
that most mired of pivotings,
and our mouths fill with three
names that can't find their meanings,
theirs, and before we know it, also
ours, and we pull up more tightly
around us the coverings of
full moonlight that fall down
now from unrepeatable life
on bodies of mother and father
and three children, and a fourth,
sleeping, quite long ago.

A Milk Bottle

A tiny creature moves
through the tide pool, holding up
its little fortress foretelling
our tragedies; another clamps
itself down to the stone. A sea anemone
sucks at my finger, mildly, I can just
feel it, though it may mean to kill—no,
it might say, to receive of me
more life. All these creatures
even half made of stone seem to thrill
to altered existences. As we do ourselves,
who advance so far, then stop, then creep
a little, stop, gasp—breath
is the bright shell
of the life-wish encasing us—gasp
it all in again, on seeing that
any time would be OK
to disappear back into all things—as when
lovers wake up at night and see
tears in each other's eyes and think, *Yes,*
but it doesn't matter, already
we will have lived forever. Yes,
if we could do that: separate
time from happiness, skim off
the molecules scattered
throughout our flesh that remember,
fling them at non-conscious things,
who may always have craved them . . . It's funny,
I seem actually to remember one certain
quart of milk that has just finished
clinking against one of its brethren
in the milkman's great hand and stands
freeing itself from itself on the rotting
doorstep in Pawtucket in 1932; then it is
picked up and taken indoors

by one in whom time hasn't yet
woven all its tangles. The bottle
will have shattered by now
in the decay of its music. And now,
by the tide pool, a sea eagle rings
its glass voice down into the sea
the sea's creatures transfigure over and over.
Around us the meantime is already overflowing.
Wherever I turn its own almost-invisibility
Streams and sparkles over everything.

FROM

The Past

1985

The Road Between Here and There

Here I heard the snorting of hogs trying to re-enter the underearth.
Here I came into the curve too fast, on ice, and touched the brake
 pedal and sailed into the pasture.
Here I stopped the car and snoozed while two small children
 crawled all over me.
Here I reread *Moby Dick*, skipping big chunks, skimming others, in
 a single day, while Maud and Fergus fished.
Here I abandoned the car because of a clonk in the motor and
 hitchhiked (which in those days in Vermont meant walking the
 whole way with a limp) all the way to a garage, where I passed
 the afternoon with ex-loggers who had stopped by to oil the
 joints of their artificial limbs and talk.
Here a barn burned down to the snow. "Friction," one of the ex-
 loggers said. "Friction?" "Yup, the mortgage, rubbin' against
 the insurance policy."
Here I went eighty but was in no danger of arrest, for I was blessed-
 speeding, trying to get home to see my children before they
 slept.
Here I bought speckled brown eggs with bits of straw shitted to them.
Here I brought home in the back seat two piglets who rummaged
 inside the burlap sack like pregnancy itself.
Here I heard again on the car radio Handel's concerto transcribed
 for harp and lute, which Inés played to me the first time,
 making me want to drive after it and hear it forever.
Here I sat on a boulder by the winter-steaming river and put my
 head in my hands and considered time—which is next to
 nothing, merely what vanishes, and yet can make one's elbows
 nearly pierce one's thighs.
Here I forgot how to sing in the old way and listened to frogs at dusk.
Here the local fortune teller took my hand and said, "What is still
 possible is inspired work, faithfulness to a few, and a last love,
 which, being last, will be like looking up and seeing the
 parachute opening up in a shower of gold."
Here is the chimney standing up by itself and falling down, which
 tells you you approach the end of the road between here and
 there.

Here I arrive there.

Here I must turn around and go back and on the way back look
carefully to left and to right.

For when the spaces along the road between here and there are all used
up, that's it.

Conception

Having crowed the seed
of the child of his heart
into the egg of the child
of her heart, in the dark
middle of the night, as cocks
sometimes cry out to a light
not yet visible to the rest,
and lying there with cock
shrugging its way out of her,
and rising back through phases
of identity, he hears her
say, "Yes, I am two now,
and with you, three."

The Sow Piglet's Escapes

When the little sow piglet squirmed free,
Gus and I ran her all the way down to the swamp
and lunged and floundered and fell full-length
on our bellies stretching for her, and got her,
and lay there, all three shining with swamp slime,
she yelping, I laughing, Gus gasping and gasping—
it was then I knew he would die soon.
She made her second escape on the one day
when she was big enough to dig an escape hole
and still small enough to squeeze through it.
Every day I took a bucket of meal up to her plot
of rooted-up ground in the woods, until
one day there she stood, waiting for me,
the wild beast evidently all mealed out of her.
She trotted over and let me stroke her back
and, dribbling corn down her chin, put up her little worried face
as if to remind me not to forget to recapture her—
though, really, a pig's special alertness to death
ought to have told her: in Sheffield the *dolce vita*
leads to the Lyndonville butcher. When I seized her
she wriggled hard and cried *oui oui oui* all the way home.

The Olive Wood Fire

When Fergus woke crying at night
I would carry him from his crib
to the rocking chair and sit holding him
before the fire of thousand-year-old olive wood.
Sometimes, for reasons I never knew
and he has forgotten, even after his bottle the big tears
would keep on rolling down his big cheeks
—the left cheek always more brilliant than the right—
and we would sit, some nights for hours, rocking
in the light eking itself out of the ancient wood,
and hold each other against the darkness,
his close behind and far away in the future,
mine I imagined all around.
One such time, fallen half-asleep myself,
I thought I heard a scream
—a flier crying out in horror
as he dropped fire on he didn't know what or whom,
or else a child thus set aflame—
and sat up alert. The olive wood fire
had burned low. In my arms lay Fergus,
fast asleep, left cheek glowing, God.

The Frog Pond

In those first years I came down
often to the frog pond—once called,
before the earthen dam wore away,
the farm pond—to bathe, wading out
and standing on a rock up to my knees
in pond water, which I saucepanned over me—
and doing it quickly because of the leeches,
who need but minutes to know you're there—
or to read the mail or to scribble
or to loaf and think, sometimes
of the future, while the one deerfly
that torments everyone who walks out in Vermont
in July—smack it dead as often
as one will—orbited about my head.
Then the beavers arrived, the waters rose,
and the frog pond became the beaver pond.
A year later a sunken rowboat surfaced,
sheet metal nailed all around it
to hold the hull boards in place
while they rotted. The four
of us would oar, pole, and bail
a few feet above the underwater green bank
where a man used to sit and think
and look up and seem to see four people
up here oaring and poling and bailing
above him: the man *seems* happy,
the two children laugh and splash,
a slight shadow crosses the woman's face.
Then one spring the beavers disappeared—
trapped off, or else because they'd eaten all
the edible trees—and soon this pond,
like the next, and the one after that,
will flow off, leaving behind its print
in the woods, a sudden green meadow
with gleams of sky meandering through it.

The man who lies propped up
on an elbow, scribbling, will be older
and will remember the pond as it was then,
writhing with leeches and overflown
by the straight blue bodies of dragonflies,
and will think of small children
grown up and of true love broken
and will sit up abruptly and swat
the hard-biting deerfly on his head,
crushing it into his hair, as he has done before.

Prayer

Whatever happens. Whatever
what is is is what
I want. Only that. But that.

Fire in Luna Park

The screaming produced by the great fright machines—
one like a dough beater that lifts, whirls, plunges the victims
        strapped to its arms,
one a huge fluted pan that tries to fling its passengers off the earth,
one that holds its riders upside down and pummels them until the
        screams pour out freely,
and above them the roller coaster, which creeps seemingly lost
        among its struts and braces before it plunges,
and under them the Ghost Train that jerks through dark tunnels
        here and there suddenly lighted by fluorescent bones—
has fallen still today.

To us who live on Lavender Bay,
once Hulk Bay, before that perhaps few now know what,
it seemed the same easily frightened, big-lunged screamer cried out
        in mock terror each night across the water, and we hardly
        heard and took no notice.
But last night the shrieks of actual terror pierced through our
        laughter, and kept at it, until we sat up startled.

The Ghost Train, now carrying seven souls and the baffled grief of
        families,
has no special destination,
but, looking for forgetfulness, must worm forward, twist, backtrack
        through the natural world,
where all are born, all suffer, and many scream,
and no one is healed but gathered and used again.

Cemetery Angels

On these cold days
they stand over
our dead, who will
erupt into flower as soon
as memory and human shape
rot out of them, each bent
forward and with wings
partly opened as though
warming itself at a fire.

On the Oregon Coast

In memoriam Richard Hugo

Six or seven rows of waves struggle landward.
The wind batters a pewtery sheen on the valleys between them.
Much of each wave making its way in gets blown back out to sea.
The bass rumble of sea stones audible under their outrush itself blows
out to sea.
A log maybe thirty feet long and six across at the fat end gets up and
trundles down the beach.
Like a dog fetching a stick, it flops unhesitatingly into the water.
An enormous wave at once sends it wallowing back up the beach.
It comes to rest among other lost logs, almost panting.
Sure enough, in a few minutes it trundles down the beach again.
The last time I was on this coast Richard Hugo and I had dinner together
north of here, in a restaurant over the sea.
The conversation came around to personification.
We agreed that eighteenth- and nineteenth-century poets almost *had* to
personify, it was like mouth-to-mouth resuscitation, the only way
they could think up to keep the world from becoming dead matter.
And that as post-Darwinians it was up to us to anthropomorphize the
world less and animalize, vegetablize, and mineralize ourselves
more.
We didn't know if pre-Darwinian language would let us.
Our talk turned to James Wright, how his confabulations with reptiles,
spiders, and insects drifted him back through the evolutionary
stages.
When a group of people get up from a table, the table doesn't know
which way any of them will go.
James Wright went back to the end. So did Richard Hugo.
The waves swaffing in burst up through their crests and fly very brilliant
back out to sea.
The log gets up yet again, rolls and bounces down the beach, and plunges
as though for good into the water.

First Day of the Future

They always seem to come up
on the future, these cold, earthly dawns;
the whiteness and the blackness
make the flesh shiver as though it's starting to break.
But so far it's just another day they illuminate
of the permanent present. Except for today.
A motorboat sets out across the bay,
a transfiguring spirit, its little puffy gasps
of disintegration collected
and hymned out in a pure purr of dominion.
In the stillness again the shore lights remember
the dimensions of the black water.
I don't know about this new life.
Even though I burned the ashes of its flag again and again
and set fire to the ticket that might have conscripted me into its ranks
 forever,
and squandered my talents composing my emigration papers,
I think I want to go back now and live again in the present time, back
 there
where someone milks a cow and jets of intensest nourishment go
 squawking into a pail,
where someone is hammering, a bit of steel at the end of a stick hitting
 a bit of steel, in the archaic stillness of an afternoon,
or somebody else saws a board, back and forth, like hard labor
in the lungs of one who refuses to come to the very end.
But I guess I'm here. So I must take care. For here
one has to keep facing the right way, or one sees one dies, and one dies.

The Fundamental Project of Technology

"A *flash! A white flash sparkled!*"
— Tatsuichiro Akizuki, *Concentric Circles of Death*

Under glass: glass dishes that changed
in color; pieces of transformed beer bottles;
a household iron; bundles of wire become solid
lumps of iron; a pair of pliers; a ring of skull-
bone fused to the inside of a helmet; eyeglasses
taken off the eyes of an eyewitness, without glass,
which vanished, when a white flash sparkled.

An old man, possibly a soldier back then,
now simply someone who will die soon,
sucks at the cigarette dangling from his lip, peers
at the uniform, scorched, of some tiniest schoolboy,
sighs out bluish mists of his own ashes over
a pressed tin lunch box well crushed back then when
the future first learned, in a white flash, to jerk tears.

On the bridge outside, in navy black, a group
of schoolchildren line up, hold it, grin at a flash-pop,
scatter like pigeons across grass, see a stranger, cry
hello! hello! hello! and soon *bye-bye! bye-bye! bye-bye!*
having pecked up the greetings that fell half unspoken
and the going-sayings that those who went the day
it happened a white flash sparkled did not get to say.

If all a city's faces were to shrink back all at once
from their skulls, would a new sound come into existence,
audible above moans eaves extract from wind that smooths
the grass on graves, or raspings heart's-blood greases still,
or wails infants trill born already skillful at the grandpa's rattle,
or infra-screams bitter-knowledge's speechlessness
memorized, at that white flash, inside closed-forever mouths?

To de-animalize human mentality, to purge it
of obsolete characteristics, in particular of death,
which foreknowledge terrorizes the contents of skulls with,
is the fundamental project of technology; however,
even *pseudologica fantastica*'s mechanisms require that
to establish deathlessness it is necessary to eliminate
those who die; a task become conceivable, when a white flash sparkled.

Unlike the trees of home, which continuously evaporate
along the skyline, these trees have been enticed down
into eternity here. No one can say which gods they enshrine.
Does it matter? Awareness of ignorance is as devout
as knowledge of knowledge. Or more so. Even though not knowing,
sometimes we weep, from surplus of gratitude, even though knowing,
twice already on earth sparkled a flash, a white flash.

The children go away. By nature they do. And by memory,
in scorched uniforms, holding tiny crushed lunch tins.
All the ecstasy-groans of each night call them back, satori
their ghostliness back into the ashes, in the momentary shrines,
the thankfulness of arms, from which they will go
again and again, until the day flashes and no one lives
to look back and say, a flash, a white flash sparkled.

The Waking

What has just happened between the lovers,
who lie now in love-sleep under the owls' calls,
call, answer, back and forth, and so on,
until one, calling faster, overtakes the other
and the two whoo together in one
shimmering harmonic—is called "lovemaking."
Lovers who come exalted to their trysts,
who approach from opposite directions
along a path by the sea, through the pines,
meet, embrace, go up from the sea,
lie crushed into each other under
the sky half golden, half deep-blueing
its moon and stars into shining, know
they don't "make" love, but are earth-creatures
who live and—here maybe no other word will do—
fuck one another forever if possible across the stars.
An ancient word, formed perhaps before
the sacred and the profane had split apart,
when the tongue was like the flame of the heart
in the mouth, and lighted each word
as it was spoken, to remind it
to remember; as when flamingos
change feeding places on a marsh,
and there is a moment, after the first to fly
puts its head into the water in the new place
and before in the old place the last to fly
lifts out its head to see the rest have flown,
when, scattered with pink bodies, the sky
is one vast remembering. They still hear,
in sleep, the steady crushing and uncrushing
of bedsprings; they imagine a sonata in which
violins' lines draw the writhings and shiftings.
They lie with heads touching, thinking
themselves back across the blackness.

When dawn touches the bed their bodies re-form,
heaps of golden matter sieved
out of the night. The bed, caressed threadbare,
worn almost away, is now more than ever
the place where such light as humans
shine with seeps up into us. The eyelids,
which love the eyes and lie on them to sleep,
open. *This is a bed. That is a fireplace.*
That is last morning's breakfast tray
which nobody has yet bothered to take away.
This face, too alive with feeling to survive past
the world in which it is said, "Ni vous
sans moi, ni moi sans vous," so unguarded
this day might be breaking in the Middle Ages,
is the illusion fateful randomness chooses
to beam into existence, now, on this pillow.
In a ray of sun the lovers see motes cross,
mingle, collide, lose their way, in this puff
of ecstatic dust. Tears overfill their eyes,
wet their faces, drain quickly away
into their smiles. One leg hangs off the bed.
He is still inside her. His big toe
sticks into the pot of strawberry jam. "Oh migod!"
They kiss while laughing and hit teeth
and remember they are bones and laugh
naturally again. The feeling, perhaps
it is only a feeling, perhaps mostly due
to living only in the overlapping lifetimes
of dying things, that time starts up,
comes over them. They get up, put on clothes,
go out. They are not in the street yet,
however, but for a few moments longer
still in their elsewhere, beside a river,
with their arms around each other, in the aura
earth has when it remembers its former beauty.
An ambulance sirens a bandage-stiffened
body toward St. Vincent's. A police car
running the red lights parodies
in high pitch the owls of paradise. The lovers

enter the ordinary day the ordinary world
providentially provides. Their pockets ring.
Good. For now askers and beggarmen
come up to them needing change for breakfast.

That Silent Evening

I will go back to that silent evening
when we lay together and talked in silent voices,
while outside slow lumps of soft snow
fell, hushing as they got near the ground,
with a fire in the room, in which centuries
of tree went up in continuous ghost-giving-up,
without a crackle, into morning light.
Not until what hastens went slower did we sleep.
When we got home we turned and looked back
at our tracks twining out of the woods,
where the branches we brushed against let fall
puffs of sparkling snow, quickly, in silence,
like stolen kisses, and where the *scritch scritch scritch*
among the trees, which is the sound that dies
inside the sparks from the wedge when the sledge
hits it off center telling everything inside
it is fire, jumped to a black branch, puffed up
but without arms and so to our eyes lonesome,
and yet also—how can we know this?—*happy!*
in shape of chickadee. Lying still in snow,
not iron-willed, like railroad tracks, willing
not to meet until heaven, but here and there
treading slubby kissing stops, our tracks
wobble across the snow their long scratch.
So many things that happen here are really little more,
if even that, than a scratch, too. Words, in our mouths,
are almost ready, already, to bandage the one
whom the *scritch scritch scritch*, meaning *if how when*
we might lose each other, scratches scratches scratches
from this moment to that. Then I will go back
to that silent evening, when the past just managed
to overlap the future, if only by a trace,
and the light doubles and casts
through the dark a sparkling that heavens the earth.

When One Has Lived
a Long Time Alone

1990

The Tragedy of Bricks

1

The twelve-noon whistle groans out
its puff of steam partway up the smokestack.
Out of the brickwork the lace-workers
carry their empty black lunch-stomachs.
The noontime composition features
that one blurry bass note
in concert with the tenor of the stomachs.
The used-up lace-worker, who is about a hundred,
bicycles past, suctions together
mouth-matter, tongue-hurls it at the mill,
rattles away. The trajectory of gold rowels
its arc of contempt across a boy's memory.

2

Overhead the sea blows upside down across Rhode Island.
slub clump slub clump
Charlie drops out. Carl steps in.
slub clump
No hitch in the sequence.
Paddy stands down. Otto jumps up.
Otto in his lifetime clumped into place seven million bricks,
fell from the scaffolding,
clump.
slub clump slub clump
Jake takes over, slubs mortar onto brick, clumps brick onto
        mortar.
Does this. Does it again.
Topples over. No pause.
René appears. Homer collapses. Angelo springs up. No break in the
        rhythm.
slub clump slub clump
They wear in they wear out.
They lay the bricks that build the mills
that shock the Blackstone River into yellow froth.

3

Here come the joggers.
I am sixty-one. The joggers are approximately very young.
They run for fun through a world where everyone used to lay bricks for
    work.
Their faces tell there is a hell and they will reach it.

4

At the blast of the last whistle
the lace-workers straggle out again
from under the tragedy of bricks.
Some stand at the trolley stop, some trudge off,
some sit between two disks of piano wire
and, walking in air, wobble into the dusk.

5

A boy born among bricks
walks beside the brick walls.
Under his steps the packed snow
sounds the small crushed shrieks
of the former bricklayers who lie
stacked somewhere hereabout.
One of them patrols the roof of the mill,
carrying a lantern, like a father,
which has a tongue in it
that does not speak, like a father.
He is there to make sure no brick
fails in its duty. Suddenly the full
moon lays out across the imperfect
world everything's grave.
slub clump slub clump.
The boy knows his father and mother
will disappear before the least brick cracks
or tells its story: an order of going
formerly known as infernal corrosion.
Up in the future they are laying the footing
for the construction of the neutron bomb,
which evaporates the living forms
and spares the bricks and the mortar.

The Cat

The first thing that happened
was that somebody borrowed the Jeep,
drove fifty feet, went off the road.
The cat may have stuck a tire iron
or baseball bat into the steering wheel.
I don't know if it did or didn't.
I do know—I don't dare say it aloud—
when the cat is around something goes wrong.
Why doesn't our host forewarn us? Well,
he tries. He gives each guest on arrival
a set of instructions about the cat.
I never was able to read mine,
for the cat was watching when I got it,
and I stuck it in my pocket to read later,
but the cat saw, leapt at me, nearly
knocked me down, clawed at the pocket,
would have ripped my clothes off
if I had not handed it over.
The guest book contains the name
of the young woman who was my friend,
who brought me here in the first place,
who is the reason I have come back,
to try to find out what became of her.
But no one will tell me anything.
Except tonight, my final evening,
at dinner, the host says, "There is
someone . . . someone . . . a woman . . .
in your life . . ." I know he means her,
but why the present tense? "Whom you have in . . ."
The next word sounds like "blurrarree"
but it could be "slavery." "Well, yes,"
I say. "Yes, but where is the cat?"
"It is an awful thing you are doing,"
he goes on. "Quite awful." "But who?"
I protest. "What are you talking about?"
"The cat," he says. "When you lock her up

she becomes dangerous." "The cat?
What cat?" I remember the kitten saved
out of the burlap sack, I was
mothering or fathering her, my father
or mother said, "Stop smothering her."
Now an electric force grabs my feet.
I see it has seized my host's, too —
he is standing up, his hands are flopping
in front of him. "What is it?" I whisper.
"I'm washing the dishes," he says.
"O my God," I think.
"I'm washing the dishes," he repeats.
I realize he is trying to get the cat to believe
he is not in a seizure but washing the dishes.
If either of us lets on about the seizure
it is certain the cat will kill us both.

Oatmeal

I eat oatmeal for breakfast.
I make it on the hot plate and put skimmed milk on it.
I eat it alone.
I am aware it is not good to eat oatmeal alone.
Its consistency is such that it is better for your mental health if
    somebody eats it with you.
That is why I often think up an imaginary companion to have
    breakfast with.
Possibly it is even worse to eat oatmeal with an imaginary companion.
Nevertheless, yesterday morning, I ate my oatmeal with John Keats.
Keats said I was right to invite him: due to its glutinous texture, gluey
    lumpishness, hint of slime, and unusual willingness to
    disintegrate, oatmeal must never be eaten alone.
He said it is perfectly OK, however, to eat it with an imaginary
    companion,
and he himself had enjoyed memorable porridges with Edmund
    Spenser and John Milton.
He also told me about writing the "Ode to a Nightingale."
He wrote it quickly, he said, on scraps of paper, which he then stuck in
    his pocket,
but when he got home he couldn't figure out the order of the
    stanzas, and he and a friend spread the papers on a table, and
    they made some sense of them, but he isn't sure to this day if
    they got it right.
He still wonders about the occasional sense of drift between stanzas,
and the way here and there a line will go into the configuration of a
    Moslem at prayer, then raise itself up and peer about, then
    lay itself down slightly off the mark, causing the poem to move
    forward with God's reckless wobble.
He said someone told him that later in life Wordsworth heard about
    the scraps of paper on the table, and tried shuffling some stanzas
    of his own, but only made matters worse.
When breakfast was over, John recited "To Autumn."
He recited it slowly, with much feeling, and he articulated the words
    lovingly, and his odd accent sounded sweet.

He didn't offer the story of writing "To Autumn," I doubt if there is
    much of one.
But he did say the sight of a just-harvested oat field got him started
    on it
and two of the lines, "For Summer has o'er-brimmed their clammy
    cells" and "Thou watchest the last oozings hours by hours," came
    to him while eating oatmeal alone.
I can see him—drawing a spoon through the stuff, gazing into the
    glimmering furrows, muttering—and it occurs to me:
maybe there is no sublime, only the shining of the amnion's tatters.
For supper tonight I am going to have a baked potato left over from
    lunch.
I'm aware that a leftover baked potato can be damp, slippery, and
    simultaneously gummy and crumbly,
and therefore I'm going to invite Patrick Kavanagh to join me.

The Perch

There is a fork in a branch
of an ancient, enormous maple,
one of a grove of such trees,
where I climb sometimes and sit and look out
over miles of valleys and low hills.
Today on skis I took a friend
to show her the trees. We set out
down the road, turned in at
the lane which a few weeks ago,
when the trees were almost empty
and the November snows had not yet come,
lay thickly covered in bright red
and yellow leaves, crossed the swamp,
passed the cellar hole holding
the remains of the 1850s farmhouse
that had slid down into it by stages
in the thirties and forties, followed
the overgrown logging road
and came to the trees. I climbed up
to the perch, and this time looked
not into the distance but at
the tree itself, its trunk
contorted by the terrible struggle
of that time when it had its hard time.
After the trauma it grows less solid.
It may be some such time now comes upon me.
It would have to do with the unaccomplished,
and with the failing marriage
of solitude and happiness. Then a rifle
sounded, several times, quite loud,
from across the valley, percussions
of the rite of human mastery
over the earth—the most graceful,
most alert of the animals
being chosen to die. I looked

to see if my friend had heard,
but she was stepping about on her skis,
studying the trees, smiling to herself,
her lips still filled, for all
we had drained them, with hundreds
and thousands of kisses. Just then
she looked up—the way, from low
to high, the god blesses—and the blue
of her eyes shone out of the black
and white of bark and snow, as lovers
who are walking on a freezing day
touch icy cheek to icy cheek,
kiss, then shudder to discover
the heat waiting inside their mouths.

The Room

The door closes on pain and confusion.
The candle flame wavers from side to side
as though trying to break itself in half
to color the shadows too with living light.
The andante movement plays over and over
its many triplets, like farm dogs yapping
at a melody made of the gratification-cries
of cocks. I will not stay long.
Nothing in experience led me to imagine
having. Having is destroying, according
to my version of the vow of impoverishment.
But here, in this brief, waxen light,
I have, and nothing is destroyed. The flute
that guttered those owl's notes into the waste hours
of childhood joins with the piano
and they play, *Being is having*. Having
may be simply the grace of the shell
moving without hesitation, with lively pride,
down the stubborn river of woe. At the far end,
a door no one dares open begins opening.
To go through it will awaken such regret
as only closing it behind can obliterate.
The candle flame's staggering makes the room
wobble and shift—matter itself, laughing.
I can't come back. I won't change.
I have the usual capacity for wanting
what may not even exist. Don't worry.
That is dew wetting my face.
You see? Nothing that enters the room
can have only its own meaning ever again.

Last Gods

She sits naked on a boulder
a few yards out in the water.
He stands on the shore,
also naked, picking blueberries.
She calls. He turns. She opens
her legs showing him her great beauty
and smiles, a bow of lips
seeming to tie together
the ends of the earth.
Splashing her image
to pieces, he wades out
and stands before her, sunk
to the anklebones in leaf-mush
and bottom-slime—the intimacy
of the visible world. He puts
a berry in its shirt
of mist into her mouth.
She swallows it. He puts in another.
She swallows it. Over the lake
two swallows whim, juke, jink,
and when one snatches
an insect they both whirl up
and exult. He is swollen
not with ichor but with blood.
She takes him and talks him
more swollen. He kneels, opens
the dark, vertical smile
linking heaven with the underearth
and murmurs her smoothest flesh
more smooth. On top of the boulder
they join. Somewhere
a frog moans, a crow screams.
The hair of their bodies
startles up. At last they call out
in the tongue of the last gods,

who refused to go,
chose death, and shuddered
in joy and shattered in pieces,
bequeathing their cries
into the human throat. Now in the lake
two faces float, looking up
at a great maternal pine whose branches
open out in all directions
explaining everything.

Farewell

after Haydn's Symphony in F-sharp Minor

for Paul Zweig (1935–1984)

The last adagio begins.
A violinist gets up and leaves the stage.
Two cellists follow, bows held straight up, cellos dangling.
The flutist picks her way lifting her flute high as if to honor it for its
        pure hollow notes during the incessant rubbing.
Soon the bassoonist leaves, then the bass fiddler.
The fortepiano player abandons the black, closeted contraption and
        walks off shaking her fingers.

On going, each player stoops at the music stand and puffs
the flame off the top of the stalk of wax
in which fireweed, flame azalea, dense blazing star stored it a summer
        ago,
adding that quantity of darkness to the hall
and the same of light
to the elsewhere where the players reassemble,
like birds in a beech and hemlock forest just before first light,
and wait for the oboist to arrive with her reliable A,
so they can tune and play
the phrases inside flames wobbling on top of stems in the field,
and in greenish sparks of grass-sex of fireflies
and in gnats murmuring past in a spectral bunch,
and in crickets who would saw themselves apart to sing,
and in the golden finch atop the mountain ash, whose roots feed in the
        mouths of past singers.

By ones, the way we wash up on this unmusical shore,
and by twos, the way we pass into the ark each time the world begins,
the orchestra diminishes, until only two are left: violinists
who half face each other, friends who have figured out what they have
        figured out by sounding it upon the other,
and scathe the final phrases.

In the huge darkness above the stage I imagine
the face, very magnified, of my late dear friend Paul Zweig,
who went away, into Eternity's Woods, under a double singing of birds,
saying something like, "Let the limits of knowing stretch and diaphanize:
knowledge that leads to purer ignorance
gives the falling trajectory its grace."

Goodbye, dear friend.
Everything on earth, born only
moments ago, abruptly tips over
and is dragged, as if by mistake,
back into the chaotic inevitable.
Even the meantime, which is the holy time
of being on earth in simultaneous lifetimes, ends.

This is one of its endings.
The violinists drag their ignorant bows across
their know-nothing strings
a last time, the last
of the adagio flies out through the f-holes.
The audience straggles from the hall and at once disappears.
For myself I go on foot on Seventh Avenue
down to the small bent streets of the Village.
From ahead of me comes a *hic* of somebody drunk,
then a *nunc*, perhaps of a head bumping against a lamppost or scaffolding.

When One Has Lived a Long Time Alone

1

When one has lived a long time alone,
one refrains from swatting the fly
and lets him go, and one is slow to strike
the mosquito, though more than willing to slap
the flesh under her, and one hoists the toad
from the pit too deep to hop out of
and carries him to the grass, without minding
the poisoned urine he slicks his body with,
and one envelops, in a towel, the swift
who fell down the chimney and knocks herself
against window glass, and releases her outside
and watches her fly free, a life line flung at reality,
when one has lived a long time alone.

2

When one has lived a long time alone,
one grabs the snake behind the head
and holds him until he stops trying to stick
the orange tongue—which forks at the end
into black filaments and flashes out
like a fire-eater's breaths and bears little
resemblance to the pimpled pink lump
that mostly dozes inside the human mouth—
into one's flesh, and clamps it between his jaws,
letting the gaudy tips show, as children do
when concentrating, and as very likely
one does oneself, without knowing it,
when one has lived a long time alone.

3

When one has lived a long time alone,
among regrets so immense the past occupies
nearly all the room there is in consciousness,
one notices in the snake's eyes, which see behind
without giving any less attention to the future,
the opaque, milky-blue cloudiness that comes
when the snake is about to throw its skin
and become new—meanwhile continuing,
of course, to grow old—the same *bleu passé*
that bleaches the corneas of the blue-eyed
when they lie back at the end and look for heaven,
a fading one suspects means they don't find it,
when one has lived a long time alone.

4

When one has lived a long time alone,
one falls to poring upon a creature,
contrasting its eternity's-face to one's own
full of hours, taking note of the differences,
exaggerating them, making them everything,
until the other is utterly other, and then,
with hard effort, probably with tongue sticking out,
going over each difference again and this time
canceling it, until nothing is left but likeness
and suddenly oneness, and...minutes later
one starts awake, taken aback at how unresistingly
one drops off into the bliss of kinship,
when one has lived a long time alone.

5

When one has lived a long time alone
and listens at morning to mourning doves
sound their kyrie eleison, or to the small thing
spiritualizing upon a twig cry, "pewit-phoebe!"
or to grasshoppers scratch their thighs' needfire
awake, or to peabody birds at midday send their
schoolboys' whistlings across the field, and at dusk,
their undamped chinks, as from marble cutters' chisels,
or at nightfall to polliwogs just rearranged into frogs
raise their ave verum corpus — listens to those
who hop or fly call down upon us the mercy
of other tongues — one hears them as inner voices,
when one has lived a long time alone.

6

When one has lived a long time alone,
one knows that consciousness consummates,
and as the most self-conscious one among these
others uttering their seemingly compulsory cries—
the least flycatcher witching up "che-bec!"
or red-headed woodpecker clanging out his tunes
from a metal roof gutter, or ruffed grouse drumming
"thrump thrump thrump thrump-thrump-
thrump-thrump-rup-rup-rup-rup-rup-r-r-r-r-r-r"
deep in the woods, all of them in time's unfolding
trying to cry themselves into self-knowing—
one knows one is here to hear them into shining,
when one has lived a long time alone.

7

When one has lived a long time alone,
one likes alike the pig, who brooks no deferment
of gratification, and the porcupine, or thorned pig,
who enters the cellar but not the house itself
because of eating down the cellar stairs on the way up,
and one likes the worm, who by bunching herself together
and expanding works her way through the ground,
no less than the butterfly, who totters full of worry
among the day lilies as they darken,
and more and more one finds one likes
any other species better than one's own,
which has gone amok, making one self-estranged,
when one has lived a long time alone.

8

When one has lived a long time alone,
sour, misanthropic, one fits to one's defiance
the satanic boast, *It is better to reign
in hell than to submit on earth*, and forgets
one's kind—the way by now the snake does,
who stops trying to get to the floor and lingers
all across one's body, slumping into its contours,
adopting its temperature—and abandons hope
of the sweetness of friendship or love,
before long can barely remember what they are,
and covets the stillness of inorganic matter,
in a self-dissolution one may not know how to halt,
when one has lived a long time alone.

9

When one has lived a long time alone,
and the hermit thrush calls and there is an answer,
and the bullfrog head half out of water utters
the cantillations he sang in his first spring,
and the snake lowers himself over the threshold
and creeps away among the stones, one sees
they all live to mate with their kind, and one knows,
after a long time of solitude, after the many steps taken
away from one's kind, toward these other kingdoms,
the hard prayer inside one's own singing
is to come back, if one can, to one's own,
a world almost lost, in the exile that deepens,
when one has lived a long time alone.

10

When one has lived a long time alone,
one wants to live again among men and women,
to return to that place where one's ties with the human
broke, where the disquiet of death and now also
of history glimmers its firelight on faces,
where the gaze of the new baby meets the gaze
of the great granny, and where lovers speak,
on lips blowsy from kissing, that language
the same in each mouth, and like birds at daybreak
blether the song that is both earth's and heaven's,
until the sun rises, and they stand
in the daylight of being made one: kingdom come,
when one has lived a long time alone.

Imperfect Thirst

1994

My Mother's R & R

She lay late in bed. Maybe she was sick,
though she was never sick. Pink flowers
were in full blossom in the wallpaper
and motes like bits of something ground up
churned in sunrays from the windows.
We climbed into bed with her.
Perhaps she needed comforting,
and she was alone, and she let us take
a breast each out of the loose slip.
"Let's make believe we're babies,"
Derry said. We put the large pink
flowers at the end of those lax breasts
into our mouths and sucked with enthusiasm.
She laughed and seemed to enjoy our play.
Perhaps intoxicated by our pleasure,
or frustrated by the failure of the milk
to flow, we sucked harder, probably
our bodies writhed, our eyes flared,
certainly she could feel our teeth.
Abruptly she took back her breasts
and sent us from the bed, two small
hungry boys enflamed and driven off
by the she-wolf. But we had got our nip,
and in the empire we would found,
we would taste all the women and expel them
one after another as they came to resemble her.

The Man in the Chair

I glanced in as I walked past
the door of the room where he sat
in the easy chair with the soiled area
along the top from the olive oil.
I think I noticed something—
a rigidity in the torso, making it
unable to settle into the cushions,
or a slackness in the neck,
causing the head to tilt forward,
or a shaking in the lifted left fist,
as though he were pushing a hammer
handle back with all his force, to pull
a spike driven nineteen years before
the end of the nineteenth century
into lignum vitae so dense the steel
may have cried out in excruciated singsong,
or an acute angle in the knees,
as if he were holding his feet inches off
the floor to keep them from a whitish
wash of mist from some freshly
dug pit simmering across it,
or the jerk of a leg, as if a hand
just then had reached up through the floor
and tried to grab it. I think I noticed,
yet I did not stop, or go in, or speak.
For his part he could not have spoken,
that day, or any day, he had a human
version of the pip, the disease that thickens
birds' vocal cords and throttles their song.
I had it too, no doubt caught from him,
and I could not speak truly except
to the beings I had invented far within.
I walked past, into my room, shut
the door, and sat down at the desk,
site of so many hours lost

passing one number through another
and drawing a little row of survivors on top,
while my mother sat across from me
catching my mistakes upside down.
I wrote, and as I did I allowed
to be audible in the room only
the scritches of the pen nib, a sound
like a rat nosing around in the dark
interior of a wall, making a nest of shreds.
All other sounds, including the words
he never said to me, my cries to him
I did not make, I forced down
through the paper, the desk, the floor,
the surface of the earth, the roof
of that dismal region where they stood,
two or three of them, who had reached up
and had him by the foot, and were pulling hard.

The Cellist

At intermission I find her backstage
still practicing the piece coming up next.
She calls it the "solo in high dreary."
Her bow niggles at the strings like a hand
stroking skin it never wanted to touch.
Probably under her scorn she is sick
that she can't do better by it. As I am,
by the dreary in me, such as the disparity
between all the tenderness I've received
and the amount I've given, and the way
I used to shrug off the imbalance
simply as how things are, as if the male
were constituted like those coffeemakers
that produce less black bitter than the quantity
of sweet clear you pour in—forgetting about
how much I spilled through unsteady walking,
and that lot I flung on the ground
in suspicion, and for fear I wasn't worthy,
and all I threw out for reasons I don't understand yet.
"Break a leg!" somebody tells her.
When she comes out, she seems nervous,
her hand shakes as she re-dog-ears the big pages
that appear about to flop over on their own.
Now she raises the bow—its flat bundle of hair
harvested from the rear ends of horses—like a whetted
scimitar she is about to draw across a throat,
and attacks. In a back alley a cat opens
its pink-ceilinged mouth, gets netted
in full yowl, clubbed, bagged, bicycled off, haggled open,
gutted, the gut squeezed down to its highest pitch,
washed, and sliced into cello strings that bring
a screaming into this duet of hair and gut.
Now she is flying—tossing back the goblets
of Saint-Amour standing empty,
half-empty, or full on the tablecloth-

like sheet music. Her knees tighten
and loosen around the big-hipped creature
wailing and groaning between them
as if locked with her in syzygial amplexus.
The music seems to rise from the crater left
when heaven was torn up and taken off the earth;
more likely it comes up through her priest's dress,
up from beneath that clump of hair that now
may be so wet with its waters, miraculous
as those the fishes multiplied in at Galilee,
that each strand wicks a portion all the way out
to its tip and fattens it into a droplet
on the bush of half notes glittering in that dark.
Now she lifts off the bow and sits back.
Her face shines with the unselfconsciousness of a cat
screaming at night and the teary radiance of one
who gives everything no matter what has been given.

Running on Silk

A man in the black twill and gold braid of a pilot
and a woman with the virginal alertness
flight attendants had in the heyday
of stewardesses go running past
as if they have just hopped off one plane
and now run to hop on another.
In the verve and fleetness of their sprint
you can see them hastening toward each other
inside themselves. The man pulls a luggage
cart with one suitcase bungeed on top of another,
and the woman . . . my God, she holds her
high heels in her hand and runs on silk!
I see us, as if preserved in the amber
of forty-year-old Tennessee sour-mash whiskey
splashed over cherishing ice, put down
our glasses, sidestep through groups
and pairs all gruffing and tinkling
to each other, slip out the door,
hoof and click down two flights of stairs.
Maybe he wonders what gives with his wife
and that unattached young man he left her
laughing with—and finds them not
where they last were, not in the kitchen,
not anywhere, and checking the hall
hears laughter jangling in the stairwell
cut off by the bang of the outside door. In the street
she pulls off her shoes and runs on stocking feet
—laughing and crying *taxiii! taxiii!*
as if we were ecstatic worshipers springing
down a beach in Bora-Bora—toward a cab
suffusing its back end in red brake light.
As I push her in, a voice behind us calls
bop! bop! like a stun gun, or a pet name.
Out the taxi's rear window I glimpse him,
stopped dead, one foot on the sidewalk,

one in the gutter, a hand on his heart. *Go! go!*
we cry to the driver. After we come together,
to our surprise, for we are strangers,
my telephone also starts making a lot
of anxious, warbling, weeping-like noises.
I put it on the floor, with a pillow on it,
and we lie back and listen with satisfaction
to the stifled rings, like dumdum bullets
meant for us, spending their force in feathers.
A heavy man trotting by knocks my leg with his bag;
he doesn't notice or care and trots on.
Could he be pursuing those two high-flyers
who have run out of sight? Will I find him, up ahead,
stopped at a just-shut departure gate, like that man
that night forty years ago, as if turned to wood
and put out by his laughing murderers to sell cigars?

The Deconstruction of Emily Dickinson

The lecture had ended when I came in,
and the professor was answering questions.
I do not know what he had been doing with her
poetry, but now he was speaking of her
as a victim of reluctant male publishers.
When the questions dwindled, I put up my hand.
I said that the ignorant meddling of the Springfield *Republican*
and the hidebound response of literary men,
and the gulf between the poetic wishfulness
then admired and her own harsh knowledge,
had let her see that her poems
would not be understood in her time;
and therefore, passionate to publish,
she vowed not to publish again. I said
I would recite a version of her vow,

> Publication—is the Auction
> Of the Mind of Man—

but before I could, the professor broke in.
"Yes," he said, "'the Auction'—'auction,' from *augere, auctum*, to
    augment, to author . . ."
"Let's hear the poem!" "The poem!" several women,
who at such a moment are more outspoken than men, shouted,
but I kept still and he kept going.
"In *auctum* the economy of the signifier is split, revealing an
    unconscious collusion in the bourgeois commodification of
    consciousness. While our author says 'no,' the unreified text says
    'yes,' yes?"
He kissed his lips together and turned to me
saying, "Now, may we hear the poem?"
I waited a moment for full effect.
Without rising to my feet, I said,
"Professor, to understand Dickinson
it may not always be necessary to uproot her words.

Why not, first, try *listening* to her?
Loyalty forbids me to recite her poem now."
No, I didn't say that—I realized
she would want me to finish him off with one wallop.
So I said, "Professor, I thought you
would welcome the words of your author.
I see you prefer to hear yourself speak."
No, I held back—for I could hear her
urging me to put outrage into my voice
and substance into my argument.
I stood up so that everyone might see
the derision in my smile. "Professor," I said,
"you live in Amherst at the end of the twentieth century.
For you 'auction' means a quaint event
where somebody coaxes out the bids
on butter churns on a summer Saturday.
Forget etymology, this is history.
In Amherst in 1860 'auction' meant
the slave auction, you dope!"
Well, I didn't say that either,
although I have said them all,
many times, in the middle of the night.
In reality, I stood up and recited the poem
like a schoolboy called upon in class.
My voice gradually weakened, and the women
who had cried out for the poem
now looked as though they were thinking
of errands to be done on the way home.
When I finished, the professor smiled.
"Thank you. So, what at first some of us may have taken as a simple
      outcry, we all now see is an ambivalent, self-subversive text."
As people got up to go, I moved
into that sanctum within me where Emily
sometimes speaks a verse, and listened
for a sign of how she felt, such as,
"Thanks—Sweet—countryman—
for wanting—to Sing out—of Me—
after all that Humbug." But she was silent.

Sheffield Ghazal 4: Driving West

A tractor-trailer carrying two dozen crushed automobiles overtakes a
  tractor-trailer carrying a dozen new.
Oil is a form of waiting.
The internal combustion engine converts the stasis of millennia into
  motion.
Cars howl on rain-wetted roads.
Airplanes rise through the downpour and throw us through the blue sky.
The idea of the airplane subverts earthly life.
Computers can deliver nuclear explosions to precisely anywhere on
  earth.
A lightning bolt is made entirely of error.
Erratic Mercurys and errant Cavaliers roam the highways.
A girl puts her head on a boy's shoulder; they are driving west.
The windshield wipers wipe, homesickness one way, wanderlust the
  other, back and forth.
This happened to your father and to you, Galway—sick to stay, longing
  to come up against the ends of the earth, and climb over.

Sheffield Ghazal 5: Passing the Cemetery

Desire and act were a combination known as sin.
The noise of a fingernail on a blackboard frightened our bones.
The stairwell on the way up to the dentist's smelled of the fire inside
    teeth.
Passing the cemetery, I wondered if the bones of the dead become
    brittle and crumbly, or if they last.
A dog would gnaw its own skeleton down to nothing, if possible.
On Holytide Wednesday a number of children came to school with
    foreheads smudged, in penance beforehand, with what will be
    left of them.
The old sermons on the evils of the flesh often caused portions of flesh
    to lose feeling, sometimes to drop off.
If we press our frontal bones to the madrone, the chill of the underearth
    passes up into us, making us shiver from within.
A deathbed repentance intended to pluck out one bright terrible thread
    could unravel a lifetime—and the lifetimes of those left behind.
Fishes are the holy land of the sea.
In them spirit is flesh, flesh spirit, the brain simply a denser place in
    the flesh.
The human brain may be the brightest place on earth.
At death the body becomes foreign substance; a person who loved you
    may wash and dress this one you believed for so long was you,
    Galway, a few embrace the memory in it, but somewhere else will
    know it and welcome it.

Parkinson's Disease

While spoon-feeding him with one hand
she holds his hand with her other hand,
or rather lets it rest on top of his,
which is permanently clenched shut.
When he turns his head away, she reaches
around and puts in the spoonful blind.
He will not accept the next morsel
until he has completely chewed this one.
His bright squint tells her he finds
the shrimp she has just put in delicious.
She strokes his head very slowly, as if
to cheer up each hair sticking up
from its root in his stricken brain.
Standing behind him, she presses
her cheek to his, kisses his jowl,
and his eyes seem to stop seeing
and do nothing but emit light.
Could heaven be a time, after we are dead,
of remembering the knowledge
flesh had from flesh? The flesh
of his face is hard, perhaps
from years spent facing down others
until they fell back, and harder
from years of being himself faced down
and falling back, and harder still
from all the while frowning
and beaming and worrying and shouting
and probably letting go in rages.
His face softens into a kind
of quizzical wince, as if one
of the other animals were working at
getting the knack of the human smile.
When picking up a cookie he uses
both thumbtips to grip it
and push it against an index finger

to secure it so that he can lift it.
She takes him to the bathroom,
and when they come out, she is facing him,
walking backwards in front of him
holding his hands, pulling him
when he stops, reminding him to step
when he forgets and starts to pitch forward.
She is leading her old father into the future
as far as they can go, and she is walking
him back into her childhood, where she stood
in bare feet on the toes of his shoes
and they foxtrotted on this same rug.
I watch them closely: she could be teaching him
the last steps that one day she may teach me.
At this moment, he glints and shines,
as if it will be only a small dislocation
for him to pass from this paradise into the next.

Rapture

I can feel she has got out of bed.
That means it is seven A.M.
I have been lying with eyes shut,
thinking, or possibly dreaming,
of how she might look if, at breakfast,
I spoke about the hidden place in her
which, to me, is like a soprano's tremolo,
and right then, over toast and bramble jelly,
if such things are possible, she came.
I imagine she would show it while trying to conceal it.
I imagine her hair would fall about her face
and she would become apparently downcast,
as she does at a concert when she is moved.
The hypnopompic play passes, and I open my eyes
and there she is, next to the bed,
bending to a low drawer, picking over
various small smooth black, white,
and pink items of underwear. She bends
so low her back runs parallel to the earth,
but there is no sway in it, there is little burden, the day has hardly
        begun.
The two mounds of muscles for walking, leaping, lovemaking,
lift toward the east—what can I say?
Simile is useless; there is nothing like them on earth.
Her breasts fall full; the nipples
are deep pink in the glare shining up through the iron bars
of the gate under the earth where those who could not love
press, wanting to be born again.
I reach out and take her wrist
and she falls back into bed and at once starts unbuttoning my pajamas.
Later, when I open my eyes, there she is again,
rummaging in the same low drawer.
The clock shows eight. Hmmm.
With huge, silent effort of great,
mounded muscles the earth has been turning.

She takes a piece of silken cloth
from the drawer and stands up. Under the falls
of hair her face has become quiet and downcast,
as if she will be, all day among strangers,
looking down inside herself at our rapture.

Flies

Walt Whitman noticed a group of them
suspended near his writing table at lunchtime;
at sunset he looked up and there they still were,
"balancing in the air in the centre of the room, darting athwart, up and
    down, casting swift shadows in specks on the opposite wall where
    the shine is."
When a person sits concentrating hard,
flies often collect in one spot, in a little bunch,
not far from that person's brain, and fly through each other.
The next day you can see them in a shaft of sun
in the barn, going over an intricacy.
Sometimes they alight on my writing-fingers
as I form letters that look like drawings of them,
or sit on the typewriter watching the keys hit,
perhaps with some of the alert misapprehension
of my mother, when I was in high school,
at the sporadic clacking coming from my room.
Karl Shapiro addressed a fly:
"O hideous little bat, the size of snot."
Yesterday I killed a fly that had been trying
to crawl up a nostril and usurp a snot's niche.
On being swatted, it jettisoned itself
into my cup of coffee. When I swat and miss,
the fly sometimes flies to the fly swatter,
getting out of striking range by going deeper
inside it, like a child hugging the person who has just
struck her. Or it might alight on my head.
Miroslav Holub says that at the battle of Crécy a fly

        alighted
    on the blue tongue
    of the Duke of Clervaux.

When Emily Dickinson's dying person dies, a fly's
"Blue – uncertain stumbling Buzz" goes with her
as far as it can go. If you fire the stoves
in a closed-up house in the fall, the cluster flies,

looking groggy, will creep from their chinks
and sleeping-holes, out of seeming death.
Soon, if the sun is out, hundreds will appear,
as if getting born right there on the window glass.
When so many vibrate together, the murmur
Christopher Smart called the "honey of the air"
becomes a howl. Seiki observes in himself
what is true of me too:

> Once I kill
> A fly I find I
> Want to massacre them all.

Then Antonio Machado cries, *But . . . but . . . they*

> have rested
> upon the enchanted toy,
> upon the large closed book,
> upon the love letter,
> upon the stiffened eyelids
> of the dead.

John Clare, who came like the Baptist to prepare us
for the teachings of Darwin, tells us flies
"look like things of the mind or fairies, and seemed pleased or dull
    as the weather permits in many clean cottages, and genteel
    houses, they are allowed every liberty to creep, fly or do as they
    like, and seldom or ever do wrong, in fact they are the small or
    dwarfish portion of our own family."
James K. Baxter said New Zealand flies regard him as their *whenua,*
which in Maori means both placenta and land.
In the year of Clare's birth, William Blake asks:

> Am not I
> A fly like thee?
> Or art not thou
> A man like me?

He could not have known the tsetse spits into its bite
the trypanosome, which releases into us
a lifetime supply of sleep, even some extra,
or that the flashy, green, meat-eating botfly

needs flesh to bury its eggs in, living flesh will do,
or that his diminutive cousin, the fly
walking on the lips of his baby, scatters manure
behind him as copiously as the god Sterquilius.
Martin Luther said, "I am a bitter enemy to flies. When I open a book
       for the first time, flies land on it at once, with their hind ends, and
       choose a spot, as if they would say, 'Here we will squat, and
       besmirch this book with our excrement.'"
The wanton among us, who kill flies for our sport,
like to hear of the evil flies do. Then we swat
with more pleasure, as if we did God's work.
"Is this thy play?" Edward Taylor cries. "For why?"
I think I have a fly inside me.
It drones through me,
at three A.M., looking for what stinks,
the more stinking the better, a filth heap
old or new, some regret, or guilt, or humiliation,
and finds it, and feeds, waking me,
and I live it again. Then, with an effort
of will feeble enough if compared with my mother's
when I arrived almost too late at her deathbed
and she broke back through her last coma and spoke,
I swat at it, and it jumps up and swerves away.
I do not think this fly will ever go.
It feels like part of me, and can't leave until
I rattle out a regret sufficient to the cause
and thus close the account. Then
it could steal out and, if the stove is lit
and the fall sun bright, fly to the window
above the table, or, if the day is gloomy,
crawl up my upper lip and hole up
in that nostril at last. So I swat,
flailing at the window almost without aiming,
until the windowsill, and the big, open
Webster's First, and the desk and part of the floor
are speckled with the flies' paltry remains,
strewn thick as the human dead in the Great War.
One of them rights itself, and walks,
and seems to feel OK, and flies.
My father righted himself out of the muck
where many thousands of dead

stuck out their blue tongues. The Preacher says,
"Dead flies cause the ointment of the apothecary to send forth a stinking
    savour."
Would that muck were an ointment some chthonic
apothecary oozes up in earth's devastated places.
But no one who rights himself out of it
and walks and feels OK
is OK.
He knows something, and wants to keep others
from smelling it on him and knowing that
he is the fly in the ointment, wherever he flies.
As the treetops' shadow creeps up the window
the flies creep just ahead of it. They often
collide, and seem troubled and confused,
as though they came here for something
and have forgotten what, and keep looking anyway,
like my father, on coming to America.
When a fly stands motionless on a window pane,
I wonder if it is looking through the bottom
facets of its eye at the outdoors.
Federico García Lorca said that if
a fly buzzes inside a window,

> I think of people
> in chains.
> And I let it go free.

A fly may not always want to go free,
even if radiant heat through the barrier of glass
lets it imagine that it does. In this
it would be like my mother, in her ardor
for poetry, before she realized that poetry
was what I was up to in my life
—though not in her craving for love in her own life.
When she looked out with her blue eye I'm sure
it seemed wild and fiery there and she knew she must go.
I find it hard to think that she did not,
at some point, with her big, walker's feet, tread hard
and break through. More than once I felt
a draft of icy air. But my sisters say no.

Neverland

Bending over her bed, I saw the smile
I must have seen when gaping up from the crib.
Knowing death will come, sensing its onset,
may be a fair price for consciousness.
But looking at my sister, I wished
she could have died by surprise,
without ever knowing about death.
Too late. Wendy said, "I am in three parts.
Here on the left is red. That is pain.
On the right is yellow. That is exhaustion.
The rest is white. I don't know yet what white is."
For most people, one day everything is all right.
The next, the limbic node catches fire. The day after,
the malleus in one ear starts missing the incus.
Then the arthritic opposable thumb no longer opposes
whoever last screwed the top onto the jam jar.
Then the coraco-humeral ligament frizzles apart,
the liver speckles, the kidneys dent,
two toes lose their souls. Of course,
before things get worse, a person could run for it.
I could take off right now, climb the pure forms
that surmount time and death, follow a line
down Avenue D, make a 90° turn right on 8th Street,
90° left on C, right on 7th, left on B, then cross
to Sixth Avenue, catch the A train
to Nassau, where the A pulls up beside the Z,
get off, hop on the Z, hurtle under the river
and rise on Euclid under the stars and taste,
with my sweetheart, in perfectly circular kisses,
the actual saliva of paradise.
Then, as if Wendy suddenly understood
this flaw in me, that I could die
still wanting what is not to be had here, drink
and drink and yet have most of my thirst
intact for the water table, she opened her eyes.

"I want you to know I'm not afraid of dying,"
she said. "I just wish it didn't take so long."
Seeing her appear so young and yet begin to die
all on her own, I wanted to whisk her off.
Quickly she said, "Let's go home." From outside
in the driveway came the gargling noise
of a starter motor, and a low steady rumbling, as if
my car had turned itself on and was warming up the engine.
She closed her eyes. She was entirely white,
as if freshly powdered with twice-bleached flour.
Color flashed only when she opened her eyes.
Snow will come down next winter, in the woods;
the fallen trees will have that flesh on their bones.
When the eye of the woods opens, a bluejay shuttles.
Outside, suddenly, all was quiet,
I realized my car had shut off its engine.
Now a spot of rosiness showed in each cheek:
blushes, perhaps, at a joy she had kept from us,
from somewhere in her life, perhaps two mouths,
hers and a beloved's, near each other, like roses
sticking out of a bottle of invisible water.
She was losing the half-given, half-learned
art of speech, and it became for her a struggle
to find words, form them, position them,
quickly say them. After much effort she said,
"Now is when the point of the story changes."
After that, one eye at a time, the left listened,
and drifted, the right focused, gleamed
meanings at me, drifted. Stalwart,
the halves of the brain, especially the right.
Now, as they ratchet the box that holds
her body into the earth, a voice calls
back across the region she passes through,
a far landscape I seem to see from above,
in prolonged, even notes that swell and diminish.
Now it sounds from beneath the farthest horizon,
and now it grows faint, and now I cannot hear it.

GALWAY KINNELL is a former MacArthur fellow and has been the state poet of Vermont. In 1982 his *Selected Poems* won the Pulitzer Prize and the National Book Award. In 2002 Kinnell was awarded the Frost Medal by the Poetry Society of America. He has translated works of Bonnefoy, Lorca, Rilke, and Villon. Kinnell is Erich Maria Remarque Professor of Creative Writing at New York University. He lives in New York City and Vermont.